ACADEMIC GAMESMANSHIP

academic gamesmanship

How to make a Ph.D. pay

Pierre van den Berghe

ABELARD-SCHUMAN
LONDON NEW YORK TORONTO

ISBN 0 200 71715 4
Library of Congress Catalogue Card Number: 70-128772

LONDON	NEW YORK	TORONTO
Abelard-Schuman Limited	Abelard-Schuman Limited	Abelard-Schuman Canada Limited
8 King St. WC2	257 Park Ave. So.	228 Yorkland Blvd.

An Intext Publisher

Printed in the United States of America

To the memory of Maurice Caullery (1868-1958), zoologist and geneticist, former Sorbonne Professor, President of the French Academy of Sciences and Foreign Member of the Royal Society, my maternal grandfather and academic exemplar, who, over half a century ago, wrote as one of his 244 publications a book on *Les Universités et la Vie Scientifique aux Etats-Unis.*

Author's Notes

This is very much an insider's book. I wrote it because, as a third generation academic, I find writing the best way of expressing myself, a kind of conditioned reflex. But, of course, my debt to my colleagues is immense, for their behavior constitutes my subject matter. They are too numerous to mention, and in any case, most of them would rather not be named here, I am sure. I will make an exception, however, for my friends Edward Gross and John F. Scott, who have too good a sense of humor to mind, and who gave me the benefit of a critical reading of parts of the manuscript. The majority of my colleagues will have to be satisfied with the assurance that any resemblance between themselves and characters between these covers is *not* purely coincidental. In last analysis, this book is not directed at my peers who are, by and large, beyond redemption, but at the students who will have to decide whether to play the game for what it is worth or to use their creativity to change the rules.

My personal hope is that they will help make this book obsolete. Among my distinguished predecessors in the study of academia, I am especially indebted to Thorstein Veblen whose *Higher Learning in America* is an undeservedly neglected classic of American social science. I regard Veblen as one of the few truly great American social scientists, whose honesty and brilliance caused him to be hounded and persecuted by his more meagerly endowed colleagues.

Finally, I am grateful to my wife, Irmgard, who wisely chose the bliss of domesticity over the hustle of academia, and strongly advised me against publishing this scandalous tract under my own name. After duly considering her sound advice, I decided as usual to disregard it and to give free rein to the vanity of seeing my name in print once more. As a tenured full professor I have not got much to gain; but, then, neither do I have much to lose.

P.L.v.d.B.
Seattle, March 1970

Contents

ACADEMIC GAMESMANSHIP

»» 1 ««

The Protective Myths

The Ivory Tower is unquestionably the most pleasant microcosm in American society. Fortunately for its academic fauna, few of the other subspecies of Homo sapiens know it. And the reason for this widespread ignorance is not accidental. Like all privileged guilds, academics restrict entry into their group and wrap themselves in shrouds of protective secrecy. The first and the most important line of defense against the massive intrusion of outsiders is a set of elaborate and highly successful myths about the nature of academic life. Briefly, there are three principal myths:

1) An academic career requires superior ability.

2) The rewards, especially the material rewards, of academic life are meager.

3) Academic life is dull.

The first myth does not stand scrutiny. The distribution of academic talent, as in all professions, follows a normal curve—i.e., most professors are mediocre, a few are incompetent, and a few are intellectually superior. It is highly questionable that college professors have greater average ability than physicians, lawyers, watchmakers, plumbers, secretaries, or perhaps even army officers. Mediocrity should be no deterrent to a university career because, combined with lengthy and semiesoteric training, it ensures a sufficient level of competence to pass for erudition and profundity of thought.

Since college professors are scrutinized mostly by undergraduates (themselves a mediocre group and one which does not have the additional benefit of esoteric training), they have little to fear, except perhaps at a few selective places like Harvard or Princeton where students are often brighter than the staff. Generally, however, students cannot tell the difference between pedantry and scholarship, between glib facility and profound insight. Indeed, neither can most academics. Consequently, the myth of college professors as a formidable brain trust of eggheads is secure. The great mass of college graduates, who, more than anything else, fear being made fools of, shrink from the audacity of even contemplating an incursion into the august groves of academe after getting their sheepskins and having their photographs taken in silly flat-topped hats.

It may be argued that professors are recruited from the best students, and hence that professors are a select group. However, since professors themselves do the selection, and since school grades at any level show a perverse lack of correlation with anything else except other school grades, the validity of this argument is highly questionable. At best, it can be argued that those students with a gift for mental mimicry become professors.

The second myth—that an academic career condemns one to a life of quasi-monastic material penury—is the most ingenious of the three. In American society, where the pecuniary criterion of excellence is so important, this myth is a powerful deterrent. As many myths, this one originated in fact. In Medieval Europe, in Imperial China, and in other preindustrial societies, scholars were often reduced to the status of respectably indolent mendicants. Even in 19th century Europe and America, scholarship was not a self-supporting way of life. It was still a luxury for gentlemen with both leisure and means to invest in the pursuit of a seat in the academy, a chair at a top university, or some other mark of prestige, all the more valuable for not being *directly* purchasable like a title of nobility, a commission in the army, or a diplomatic post.

Today, however, professors need not have inherited wealth or live in garrets. They earn as good a living as other professionals with similar amounts of training, if one considers the numerous fringe benefits and the four months of annual vacation. The president of Harvard earns only a fraction of what his counterpart at General Motors does, but at that level, differences in income are almost purely symbolic. The successful professor at a major university can easily earn $25,000 to $30,000—some three times the national average. His professional income includes, besides his regular salary, consulting and lecturing fees, book and article royalties, extra salary for summer teaching or research, not to mention opportunities for free trips to exotic places, scholarships for his children, and numerous tax deductions for professional expenses. Even the young assistant professor is hardly impecunious with a starting salary of $10,000 to $12,000. In fact, he roughly *begins* life at the national average, with good prospects of doubling his income in a decade or less.

University professors earn less than physicians, but then

they do not have to work as hard or as long for their money. No other profession gives one so much security and material comfort to do what one likes at one's own pace and in nearly complete independence. As to security of tenure, it is nearly unparalleled in any other job. Academia combines the security of a large and affluent bureaucracy with the independence of "free" entrepreneurship. It is the surest road to a life of comfortable indolence if one feels so inclined, and of serene dedication to one's harmless manias if one chooses to "work."

How then, one may ask, does the myth of the indigent professor survive? The answer lies largely in the behavior of professors who, unlike most of their fellow citizens, compete with each other in *in*conspicuous consumption. Through a peculiar kind of reverse snobbery, the display of wealth is held by most professors to be a vulgar expression of material mass culture, a trap of the advertising industry and the "consumer society." They leave the flashy Chryslers and Cadillacs to low-brow prizefighters and real estate agents, and sport dusty Volkswagens or Volvos, or at least motorcars which do not *look* flashy and expensive. They would not dream of buying their wives mink stoles; they sneer at television (the "idiot box"), and if they have color sets they hide them in their bedrooms; they dress in drab, baggy clothes, cherish shoes with holes in the soles, and visit the barber at most once a month. Thus the careful affectation of a seedy look gets mistaken by the layman for financial need.

The luxuries of professors have relatively low visibility: private schools for their children, cultural trips to Europe (staying at inconspicuous hotels), theater and concert tickets, French wines, art books, record collections, recorder lessons, and other paraphernalia of the "high culture" of which academics regard themselves as the custodians. The affectation of poverty protects professors from the envy and competition of laymen, flatters their self-perception of superiority over the mass of uncouth philistines, and allows the more politically conscious among them the thrill of vicarious identification with the oppressed. They can have their cake, eat it, and yet pretend not to eat it.

The third protective myth concerns the alleged dullness of university life. Unlike the first two myths, the third one is perpetuated by laymen rather than academics. The stereotype of the professor as a dull, pedantic bookworm spending his life ruining his eyes in a dingy library or over a microscope, or boring his students in the classroom, is, of course, a caricature of reality. The professor is held to be a paragon of impracticality, removed from the "real" world of action. "Those who can, do; those who can't, teach." Although this stereotype is difficult to reconcile with the picture of the academic as a person of staggering intellect, the two views are often simultaneously held by the same laymen. Academics are disliked for their aloofness, ridiculed for their absent-mindedness, feared for their radicalism. The important thing is that to most red-blooded American boys and girls, the red-minded professor is a fairly repulsive figure. Consequently, competition for the few born into the academic caste is not very keen.

The degree to which professors succeed in shielding the mass of their compatriots from knowledge about their way of life is little short of amazing. One might suppose that undergraduates after spending four years on a campus might catch a few glimpses of what kind of animals their teachers are, but in fact very few students see through the protective myths. Professors know a good deal about student culture, but the reciprocal is not true. Teachers and students live side by side in two groups separated by a symbolic one-way window such as sociologists and social psychologists devise for their small-group experiments. Professors can observe the students, but the students see only the faintest shadows behind the metallic glare of the glass. The two groups live in different worlds, have different interests and values, and interact only in the most ritualized circumstances. How teachers maintain these protective screens on the campus will be discussed in Chapter Six.

A few students, through the intimacy of the laboratory, the office, or the bedroom penetrate the screens and get to know their teachers as persons. By emulating the behavior, tastes, and idiosyncracies of their mentors, they catch their attention, and soon get recognized as "good" students and potential recruits to academia. However, they will still have to undergo a lengthy and tedious noviciate before they are finally admitted into the priesthood. They will have to undergo the hazing and rites of passage of graduate school, the second line of defense against lay intruders. How these lean years of apprenticeship can best be survived will be the subject of Chapter Three, but before turning to that important topic, an understanding of the prestige system of academia is essential.

»» 2 ««

The Academic Pecking Order

The ingenuity displayed by man in making invidious distinctions between himself and his fellows is sufficiently great as to provide a field of specialization, and hence a livelihood for a substantial number of sociologists. The academic game cannot be played successfully without an adequate understanding of the status hierarchy or pecking order of the players. Hierarchies are the consequence of competition for scarce resources. The more you get, the higher you rank; and the higher you rank, the more you are allowed to take. Subhuman species, and some human groups, compete for basic necessities like food and sex. However, professors are too well fed to regard food as a scarce resource. Prescriptive monogamy in American society has seriously interfered with man's harem-building propensities, though, of course, modest and clandestine little ventures in that direction may occasionally be indulged in. Unlike baboons, professors cannot openly fight over the right to mount coeds on the campus green. In fact, any attempt to do so outside the privacy of one's office would be regarded as moral turpitude and a cause for dismissal.

There remain three basic commodities over which most men spend most of their lives fighting: power, wealth, and prestige. Academics fight over all three, but most of all over the last. Universities and colleges are, first and foremost, institutions in which positions are gained or improved by patting your colleagues' backs, or by deprecating their efforts, or by a judicious combination of both techniques.

This is not to say that professors are indifferent to power and wealth, but the scope for invidious distinctions on these two dimensions is not very great. The salary ratio of a full professor to a beginning assistant professor is only about two to one. How unsatisfying for a Nobel Prize winner in Physics to think of himself as only twice as good as the young Ph.D. from Kansas State who may never get anything worthwhile published. (By comparison, the head of a corporation can regard himself as twenty or thirty times as valuable as a junior executive or production engineer.)

Power also does not differentiate well enough among professors. The basic power of professors is to flunk students, and hence to affect adversely their life chances. This power is jealously guarded and shared equally by all teachers, from the most junior assistant professor to the most senile full professor. Under the guise of protecting academic freedom and professional autonomy, every teacher has despotic power over students. In the British system, this power is mitigated by external examiners and reviewed by academic Senate, but in America, the judgment of the teacher is final. A student may cajole, bribe, or seduce his or her teacher to change a grade; a dean may drop a discreet hint over the telephone that the star football player should be given a D instead of an F so that he can stay in school; but in last analysis, there is no effective redress against the arbitrary judgment of the teacher.

The trouble with this power, however, is that, since it is equally shared by all professors, it cannot serve as a basis for making invidious distinctions among them. The only kind of power that can serve that gratifying function is power over one's colleagues. Some measure of it can be acquired by becoming a departmental chairman, a dean, a provost, or a university president. By and large, the more academically mediocre a college or university is, the more powerful its administration is, and the more valued administrative posts are. The poorer community colleges and religiously affiliated schools are almost undistinguishable from high schools in this respect. In big-league academia, however, to become an administrator often entails a loss of prestige and leisure, a vast amount of uninteresting work, and only a modicum of power.

At good schools, a department chairman or a dean can have a certain amount of nuisance value to his colleagues; he can retard their promotion or deny them a "merit" increase in salary. But, actually, his power is limited because the opportunities for professors to move to a better job at another university are so great. In fact, the mere threat of resignation, judiciously used, frequently suffices to obtain what one demands as we shall see in Chapter Five. Once a professor has tenure, there is little a chairman or dean can do to him, except be an irritant, and even that is very much a two-way affair.

Luckily, there remains prestige as a basis of differentiation among professors. Here the possibilities are limitless, and professors have developed a pecking order of such scope, complexity, and subtlety as to deserve admiration. Vanity, a trait ascribed to certain male birds of bright plumage and to females of the human species who display varying portions of their epidermis on the screen or stage, is likewise the dominant characteristic of college and university teachers.

This little book cannot do justice to the intricacies of academic rankings; it can only provide a modest introduction to an extremely immodest world. Every academic belongs to at least three discrete status systems: he is a member of the larger society, of his college or university, and of the group of people who share his specialty.

In the larger society, the professor is ascribed a solid place in the upper middle class, though his unkept lawn, unwashed car, black friends, or long-haired progeny may occasionally attract the ire of his neighbors. However, even withal his status is sufficiently secure that he can afford such harmless eccentricities. In any case, most professors could not care less what their neighbors think of them, because their social life is almost exclusively confined to other academics. Whether professorial homes are grouped in a gilded ghetto as is the case in some small college towns, or physically dispersed over large metropolitan areas, professors constitute something close to an occupational caste with strict rules of commensality. There are exceptions of course. Some bored wives of civic-minded professors will canvass for the League of Women Voters or engage in some other form of do-goodism. And the more radical academics will occasionally rub shoulders with the oppressed in protest marches. But, for most academic families, the supermarket and department store are the only significant links with the outside world.

Occasionally, a professor gains notoriety in the larger society by climbing Mount Everest[1], writing a salacious book, inventing a bigger and better bomb, murdering his wife, stirring up the students, transplanting a heart, naming his dog after the president of the republic to which he has been temporarily sent as ambassador, or some such noteworthy action. Celebrity among laymen, however, is frowned upon in academia and often can only be purchased at the cost of prestige loss in the other two status systems, the ones that really count.

Professors belong to two large groups of colleagues: the staff of their college or university, and all fellow specialists in their discipline. Only the members of a given department at a given university share common membership in both of these larger groups. Thus the department is the academic habitat par excellence, the principal scene for the enactment of competition for prestige. Only fellow specialists can fully evaluate one's prestige, and one regularly interacts only with those specialists who teach at the same university. Yet, both of the larger groups contribute to a scholar's sum total of prestige in a complex and partly reciprocal fashion.

Universities and colleges, as even laymen know, are ordered in a hierarchy of prestige. The layman's hierarchy does not necessarily correspond to the academic person's evaluations. Thus, it may be socially prestigious to go to an "elite" liberal arts college tucked away in the hills of New Hampshire or Connecticut, but such places do not rank

[1] With apologies to my friend and colleague Richard Emerson, who was crazy enough to do just that.

high in the preference of most academics, except for a few snobs and eccentrics who genuinely enjoy teaching. With a remarkable degree of consensus, professors rank institutions of higher learning into a number of pyramidal categories. At the top, there are ten or twelve great universities, with the twin giants of Harvard and Berkeley among them; then one finds a further fifteen or so distinguished institutions trembling on the edge of greatness but lacking the aura of the great ones. Following is roughly a score of highly respectable schools, which however begin to show certain weaknesses especially in graduate training and facilities; then come some fifty to seventy-five colleges that do a decent job of educating undergraduates and to whose staff one can belong without having to apologize or explain where the school is located; a further 200 to 250 schools might still perhaps be described as on the right side of academic respectability, but one would rather not be there if one had a choice. Finally there is the great dismal mass of the 2000-odd institutions that are of "higher learning" only by the most charitable of definitions.[2]

The large university, whether private or public, with a well-established graduate program, a good library and research facilities, low teaching loads, and a selected undergraduate body is the most desirable. The small isolated college with heavy teaching, a poor library, and no research facilities or graduate students stands at the other extreme, especially if it is a vocationally oriented commu-

[2] This last category has been termed "academic Siberia," a designation unfair to Siberia, whose institutions of higher learning are undoubtedly of better quality. Perhaps one should speak of academic Alaska instead. The reader should excuse my refusal to name any schools (beyond the reference to Harvard and Berkeley), as doing so might adversely affect the sale of this book.

nity college or a religiously affiliated one. The "elite" liberal arts college stands somewhere in between. To join a given institution automatically places one on a prestige ladder according to the rank of the institution, and, more specifically, of one's own department among the others in the nation. Indeed, not only are colleges and universities given an over-all ranking, but in each discipline an academic will, with considerable consistency, be able to establish a rank order of departments in his field. Thus University A might have a "top ten" over-all ranking, but its chemistry department might only rank "top twenty but not top ten."

One's university affiliation pegs one at a certain level vis à vis colleagues on other campuses, but within one's institution many finer status distinctions are made. First, in a given college or university, the various departments are placed on a rough scale of intellectual distinction, and, interestingly, the order is much the same everywhere: medicine, mathematics, and the natural sciences are high status subjects, while education, agriculture, social work, and nursing rank low; the social sciences and humanities have intermediate status with yet finer distinctions between the specific fields, e.g., economics frequently ranks higher than sociology. As a general rule, the more quantitative and the less "applied" a subject is, the higher its status; and as the higher status subjects tend to attract the better students and vice versa, this prestige order frequently does reflect real qualitative differences in both staff and students.

This prestige ranking of subjects is also related to the students' assessment of the difficulty of a course. Courses known to be "gut," "snap," or "mickey mouse" have low status; thus one way a professor can enhance his status as a lecturer is to be a stiff grader. Alternatively, he can try to be a popular lecturer, a policy which calls for lenient grades and a certain histrionic flair. Reserving a discussion of teaching strategies for Chapter Six, it should be noted that the opinions of students, especially of undergraduates, have relatively little direct bearing on the teacher's prestige. Nevertheless, the person who has a reputation for being a good teacher is the object of a certain amount of envy on the part of his colleagues. (This envy is reflected in sneering remarks that X is a "crowd pleaser.") Interestingly, most professors are unwilling to grant that students are legitimate judges of their performance, yet teachers *do* compete for students, especially for graduate ones. Ability to attract a coterie of sycophantic graduate students is an important prestige symbol. And, recently, student ratings of teachers have somewhat increased the relevance of undergraduate opinion to academic prestige within the university.

On the whole, however, in conformity with Veblen's theory of conspicuous leisure, a top prestige symbol in academia is how little one teaches. The higher one's rank and the more exalted one's reputation, the fewer defiling "contact hours" one has with students, and the more senior the students. Lecturers and assistant professors typically spend nine to twelve hours a week with freshmen and sophomores; full and associate professors spend six or fewer hours with seniors and graduate students. And a few prima donnas manage to get research professorships that entail no teaching at all beyond an occasional graduate seminar.

Academic title (instructor, lecturer, assistant professor,

associate professor, etc.) is perhaps the most visible determinant of prestige within the university. To each rank belong certain rights and privileges. Tenure usually comes with promotion to an associate professorship; salary and power increase with rank though not very steeply, while work load decreases. Office space, especially where scarcity forces some "doubling up," is generally proportional to rank, and so is access to secretarial assistance. In short, the less one has to do, the better the facilities one has to do it, and the more one gets paid for it. A more detailed description of this enticing process will be reserved for Chapter Five.

So much for the main factors making for prestige competition within the university. Let us now turn to the external prestige system—the prestige determined by the recognition of colleagues in your discipline. The overwhelming majority of them are attached to other institutions and are thinly spread all over the world. Each discipline thus constitutes a vast network of people isolated from each other except during the brief ritual of the annual convention when scholars converge on some large city's Hilton Hotel for three or four days of inebriated gossip, frantic job-hunting, and unashamed prestige-mongering. The national, indeed the international, nature of this prestige system, as well as the imputed expertness of the judgments passed makes the body of fellow specialists the ultimate measure of a scholar's worth. Unless your work is known and discussed by other experts in your field, you are a strictly local figure. It is immaterial that most criticisms be adverse, as they most typically are; the important thing is that you be spoken and written about, preferably by people you have never met.

One of the surest indices of academic prestige is the frequency with which your name is cited in colleagues' publications. As important as frequency is the context in which you are quoted. It may range from an incidental footnote, to a critical paragraph, an entire article, or even a doctoral thesis or a biography. Of course, you get quoted to the extent that you publish; to this important topic we shall devote the whole of Chapter Seven.

Apart from printed evidence of scholarly status, the annual convention or meeting of the professional association is the greatest prestige show in the academic world. Conventions mean many things to many people. Ostensibly, they are a forum for the exchange of ideas and the presentation of papers on the latest advances in the discipline. In fact, this is little more than a pretext to justify the university's paying your travel expenses. To graduate students, conventions are a slave market for academic employment. More senior academics have a chance to peddle their manuscripts to publishers' representatives. Old classmates exchange gossip over cocktails. Various committees transact business. Foundation and government agents are solicited for support. All these varied and useful functions are overshadowed, however, by the fact that the annual meetings are first and foremost rituals of prestige competition. Professors strut around on the soft carpets of hotel lobbies with the assiduousness of birds of paradise in their display dances, but without even the excuse of a tangible reward such as the favors of females.

Unknown young scholars attend conventions to court the favor of the nationally known ones, and the latter in order to receive the homage of the nonentities, to bask in the sunshine of their glory, and to defend their territory against challengers. Regular attendance at conventions can actually be a substitute for publishing as a method for achieving a reputation. If the people who matter have seen you often enough, your name will be bandied about and suggested for editorial boards, offices in your professional society, and the like. After a decade of diligent attendance and proper courting of the mighty, you may find yourself an established star of a magnitude quite disproportional to your scholarly accomplishment. You will then be one of these people about whose accomplishments colleagues are understandably hazy, but whose name will nevertheless appear on a great many committees and boards. You will in fact have become the recipient of an unearned academic reputation, but as relatively few people can tell the difference between that and the *bona fide* article, the sources of your recognition are of little consequence.

Meetings are excellent barometers of professional standing. You know that you are leaving the drab herd of mere teachers of undergraduates when the following things begin to happen with increasing frequency:

1) People whom you cannot remember having ever seen claim to have met you at such and such a place.

2) Important colleagues recognize you on sight without having to cast a furtive glance at the name tag on your lapel.

3) Colleagues who have never met you read your name tag and exclaim: "Oh! I have long wanted to meet you," or "I am using your book in my class," or "I have just read your article in such-and-such journal."

4) People whom you only know slightly approach you and say: "The grapevine has it that you are unhappy at X. Would you be interested in coming to Y?"

5) Graduate students deferentially approach you as the authority on the subject on which they are writing their thesis, and ask for advice or for clarification of a fine point in your thinking.

6) You accidentally overhear your name mentioned in colleagues' conversations.

7) Your name is formally cited by colleagues reading papers. (It doesn't matter whether their comments are positive or negative.)

8) Rumors and anecdotes circulate about you. (Their nature is unimportant.)

9) Publishers' agents ask you: "Won't you write a textbook for us?"

10) Your feuds with colleagues become notorious.

11) A slight expectant hush follows your appearance in a group.

12) People approach you with greater frequency than you approach others.

13) Your own former classmates become openly envious.

If these flattering things do not begin to occur between five and ten years after getting your Ph.D., they will probably never happen. You might as well stop attending professional meetings and withdraw to the security of your college, where you can at least cut something of a figure at the faculty club and make students laugh at your jokes.

These two academic prestige systems—the one rooted in the local university and the other based on national recognition in the professional association—are intricately interconnected. Thus, in order to gain the respect of your professional peers, you must be affiliated with a respectable institution. If you are located at Apache Creek Junior College[3], you have obviously fallen by the wayside, and no self-respecting school will condescend to pull you out of the hole. Conversely, tenure and promotion at the better universities depend in good part on publication and on some test of professional recognition outside the home campus.

The principal ground on which these two forces meet is, of course, the academic department. And, since the national system is paramount, day-to-day prestige competition between members of a department consists mostly in impressing upon others how much better known than your colleagues you are outside the home university. There are several ways to do this, such as discreetly attracting your colleagues' attention to quotations from your work in the publications of others. You may even resort to some such ruse as asking your secretary to drop into a departmental meeting to let you know that you have a person-to-person call from the Under-Secretary of Defense or the Chancellor of the University of Chicago.

By far the most effective way of establishing prestige is to be frequently away from the campus on long-distance trips. The top dogs in any department are the ones who are constantly attending international conferences, giving lectures at other universities, or consulting with government or industrial firms—in short, the professorial jet set. The jet-propelled professor does almost everything except that for which he draws his salary. His undergraduates have to be content with lecture notes hastily scribbled on the back of airline menus between the martini and the crab cocktail; the university that pays his way to give a prestigious public

[3] The name is meant to be fictitious, but such a place probably does exist, in which case I proffer my apologies in advance.

lecture will have to be satisfied with a few associations of ideas hastily thrown together between planes to the accompaniment of saccharine music at O'Hare airport. Some professors even keep a mental note of their annual air mileages. The truly big-league log at least 100,000 miles (about fifteen transcontinental round-trips). Meanwhile, the graduate teaching assistants get valuable experience, and the undergraduates get what is known in polite society as the short end of the stick but what in student culture goes by a more vivid (but alas, unprintable) simile. The airborne professor is no longer simply absent-minded, he is also absent-bodied, a fleeting shadow that can occasionally be sighted picking up his mail in the departmental mail room.

Short of being physically absent from campus, prestige competition calls for at least being inaccessible, ostensibly in order to engage in prestigious work, namely research or writing. The device of the secretary to answer the phone and screen visitors is of course widely used inside and outside of academia. But only a few of the more senior professors who are departmental chairmen or have large research grants have private secretaries. So professors have devised other ways of making themselves unavailable, especially to students. They can stay at home where they can keep a nice little tax-deductible study. More ingeniously, they can have unnamed office doors where only the initiated can find them. Or else they can get lost between their multiple offices. Thus a professor can belong to both an institute and a department and have an office in each; or he can abscond to the entrails of the library where he has a cozy cubicle and cannot even be reached by telephone.

Having drawn the tantalizing picture of academic success, we must discuss the ways of getting onto the ladder in the first place, a painful subject to which we shall now turn.

»» 3 ««

The Lean Years: Apprenticeship

The most casual observer of the American campus notices that its inhabitants belong to two widely different cultures —that of professors and that of students, or more specifically of undergraduates. The two cultures are not only different; they are to a large extent antagonistic, a fact only recently discovered by student radicals. The undergraduates are the proletarians of academia—affluent proletarians to be sure, but nevertheless the large, anonymous, disenfranchised mass. The view that colleges exist for students is another of those astonishingly successful myths which professors have propagated for their own benefit.

The campus is a government of professors, for professors, and by professors.[1] Every campus has, of course, a

[1]It may be argued that administrators operate the colleges and universities, and to a large extent it is true that the mass of professors are content to let administrators run the show. However, the administrators themselves are in large part drawn from the ranks of the teaching staff, and their actual powers *vis à vis* their teaching colleagues are circumscribed by custom, the threat of resignation and protest, and other effective devices. It is best to view the administrators as a subgroup of professors, or, in Marxian terminology, the executive committee of the ruling class.

parallel body known as "student government," but clearly the term is a misnomer. Student government is mickey mouse stuff, as any politically conscious student well knows. Student elections are even more ritualistic than their adult counterparts on the national scene, and are about as meaningful (but not nearly as much fun) as football rallies or panty raids. Students do not rule themselves, much less their college or university. Much like natives under a colonial administration, they are paternalistically ruled by the campus bureaucrats acting supposedly *in loco parentis*, but in fact on behalf of the professors.

On large campuses, the sham of the "big happy family" and the "community of scholars" myths is becoming increasingly apparent. Students are more and more class-conscious and alienated. In the small liberal arts colleges which, in exchange for high tuition costs, still put up a half-way credible show of interest in students, the classically Marxian nature of the class conflict between professors and students remains hidden behind the facade of "faculty-student contact." But in fact, the smaller a school is, the more tyrannical and restrictive the authorities are toward the students who are much in the position of workers in a small, paternalistic, family firm. In the large urban campuses, students can stage a sit-down strike in the administration building; on the small, isolated, bucolic campus so dear to the academic romantics, the students are even more powerless and atomized than in the state multiversity.

Relationship to the means of production determines both class position and class conflict. The key means of production at a university is knowledge, or, at least, that which passes for such and is tested in examinations. The commonly accepted proof of knowledge is the diploma. If this were true only within the university, professors would not have much power over students. However, in our highly technocratic society, professors have been extraordinarily successful in convincing almost everybody in the larger society that college and university degrees are the best proofs of knowledge and ability that exist, and furthermore that professors are the best possible arbiters of who should get diplomas. Any American who aspires to something better than pounding away at a typewriter for $300 a month, or manning the cash register at the corner supermarket, must have a college degree[2], and college degrees (of vastly varying quality) are given exclusively by professors.

Professors, in effect, have a tight control over the life chances of the top third of the nation's manpower. While that power is diffused between hundreds of thousands of professors and thousands of schools, the knowledge factories and their professional "owners" exercise a collective monopoly of the most important means of production in "post-capitalist" societies, namely technical skills.

Young men, at any rate the vast majority of them, attend college in order to get a degree that will in turn land them an upper-level job. Young women go to college, in large part, so as to find a college-educated husband with good prospects. Educational endogamy makes it difficult for the non-college-educated girl to find a "good" husband, as any coed knows. Professors frown on such mercenary and matrimonial motives, and try to convince students that they should be interested in knowledge for its own sake. Amaz-

[2]A significant exception is the labor aristocracy of skilled trades; but then, many labor unions are much more difficult to enter than colleges.

ingly, they are successful with a minority of students who in due course become professors themselves, after a lengthy and painful process which we shall presently describe.

The two hostile classes, professors and students, meet physically in the lecture hall, but their minds and their emotions remain poles apart. The student wants to get his degree as painlessly as possible. He wants small steady cuds of easily digestible knowledge, which, in the manner of ruminants, he can regurgitate at examinations. This he wants to do in a minimum of time so as to have enough leisure to play sports, make love, or indeed—all too often—earn the money necessary to keep him in school so that later he will have an easier time earning money.

The professor, on the other hand, wants to make learning as difficult and traumatic as possible so as to restrict production of diplomas and keep up the value of his product. And the most effective device to traumatize students is to tell them that they must think for themselves, something they have been conditioned *not* to do since their infancy. Like the rat which suddenly gets an electric shock instead of a food pellet after pressing on the right lever, the student is shocked into not giving hitherto expected answers. Of course, students quickly learn that most professors do not really expect them to carry independence of mind to the extent of disagreeing with their mentors, but occasionally a peculiarly sadistic professor does actually penalize his pupils for *agreeing* uncritically with him. So the poor student never quite knows where he stands, a situation which, among laboratory rats, leads to experimental neuroses.

These profound conflicts in values and in interests between professor and student express themselves symbolically through totally different cultures. Almost everything that professors admire and like, students sneer at, and vice versa. Thus the football hero of the 1950's who was tackled by hordes of adoring coeds was seen by his professors as a primate specimen to be kept in a cage. When professors liked Bach, students studied square dancing; now that students can buy Vivaldi records at $1.98, professors turn to folk music. In the 1950's, when students wore crew cuts, professors had long hair; now something close to the reverse is true. In the 1950's "liberal" professors espoused the cause of downtrodden blacks against conservative fraternities; now the same liberals are fighting against black students on the same campuses. The twain seldom meet.

Occasionally they do, however. Sometimes the professor, in a flash of narcissistic recognition, sees in the chosen student a younger image of himself. The occasional student who shows a genuine or affected respect for knowledge for its own sake (knowledge being personified, of course, by his favorite professor) has virtually ensured himself admission into graduate school, provided he is not an out-and-out moron.

Once the student, armed with his B.A., has crossed the threshold of the graduate school, he has passed the great divide between the two classes. True, his status is ambiguous; he is still called a student, but as a research or teaching assistant he has some of the obligations of the staff (though as yet none of their privileges except the somewhat dubious ones conferred by the library). Graduate school is a no man's land between the two cultures, a purgatory before the scholarly heaven, a testing ground before admission into the priesthood. Yet, the gulf between the undergraduate and postgraduate world is much greater than between the graduate student and the professor. For though the road before him is long and arduous, and though he may fall by the wayside, the graduate student is in every respect an apprentice professor.[3]

There are basically two sets of things that a graduate student must learn if he is to conquer his Ph.D. First, he must acquire the baggage of knowledge or pedantry that his professors regard as essential for admission into their august fraternity. Second, he must learn the culture of academe. This second task is fully as important for success as the first, and fully as difficult because he has not yet been initiated into all the mysteries of the cult.

Acquisition of higher knowledge is the avowed aim of graduate school, the ostensible object of the rites of passage through which the student goes in his pursuit of the gold tassel. The pitfalls are numerous, the competition is acute, and the rate of failure is high. Only a little more than one undergraduate in ten receives the call to enter graduate school; and of those who enter, only a tenth get their doctorates. The vast majority of those who enter graduate school get an academically worthless master's degree, which entitles them to teach 15 hours a week at Pocahontas State Teachers' College.[4] In fact, at many good schools, the master's degree is a consolation prize for flunking the Ph.D. examinations. (This is referred to, in somewhat sinister analogy to cancer, as a "terminal master's.")

Most graduate departments subject their neophytes to three main spells of hazing, spread over a period ranging

[3]Of course, I am not speaking of graduate students in professional schools like Law and Medicine, which do not typically lead into academia.
[4]See footnote 2, Chapter 2.

from three to seven or more years. These tests decrease in severity but increase in ritualism as one progresses through them. First, after one or two years, students generally take a set of preliminary or qualifying examinations where there is a substantial rate of failure, or, what amounts to the same, of diagnoses as "terminal master's." At that stage, the student has typically not yet had time to establish a personal relationship with a staff patron, unless the student happens to be a sexually attractive and aggressive girl. Consequently, the student is still evaluated on criteria that bear some relationship to his intellectual potential.

Once the student is over that first hurdle, he can be nearly assured of success if he exhibits some perseverance, humility (affected or real), and understanding of departmental politics. From there on, the student will no longer be judged primarily on merit, but on his attitudes and conformity to academic culture. By the time he is ready for his second set of exams—the comprehensive or general ones at the end of his third or fourth year—professors have usually made up their minds in advance whether he should pass or fail. Generally, the cards are stacked in favor of the student who now has attached himself to one or two "major professors." These mentors now feel that the student represents a considerable investment of their precious time. In the best cases, they have a deep enough emotional commitment to the student to feel that any attack by their colleagues against the student is an attack against themselves. In most instances, this will result in the restraint of criticism, although this situation can also lead to the student becoming the innocent victim of a quarrel between his professors. We shall deal with this pitfall presently.

When the student passes the second hurdle, he has got

it made, provided he still has enough energy left to throw a thesis together, and does not antagonize his thesis director. The first draft of a thesis may be returned for revisions, but seldom is a thesis rejected outright. The final ritual of the oral defense of the dissertation is a foregone conclusion, although it affords the committee members a final chance to make the student (and indirectly his thesis director) look silly. Even if they do, it scarcely ever prevents them from granting the candidate a doctorate, and therewith a membership card into the academic fraternity.

The specialized knowledge in a discipline, which a graduate student accumulates, is a necessary but not a sufficient condition for academic progress toward the Ph.D. He must also convince his teachers that they are not wasting their time with him—i.e., that he is properly motivated and committed to the discipline, and that he will be a creditable member of his profession. In sociological jargon, he must be "acculturated" into academia and "socialized" into the norms of his professional group. The first rule of survival for the student is to size up his department, to learn its micropolitics. He must quickly learn who its influential members are; who sets the examination questions; who likes and hates whom; who the cantankerous isolates are; who derives a sadistic pleasure out of flunking students; and who the kind-hearted father figures are.

The task is by no means easy, because the graduate student typically enters his department in a state of naive ignorance and idealistic misconception about academic life. Furthermore, "professional ethics" (the rules of secrecy used in all professions to protect the members' interests against laymen) will often cause his teachers to be tight-lipped about factionalism and conflict within the department. The most worthwhile informants for the new graduate student are obviously his senior fellow students, who are no longer direct competitors but not yet full academics. Such senior students generally love to impress the younger ones with the depth of their knowledge and cynicism.

Graduate students in the same or in adjacent years are fiercely competing with each other for their professor's attention, favor, and esteem. Most professors being males, female students have an obvious advantage here, and they should make the most of it because this is the last occasion where being a woman in academia is an advantage. Generally, the academic world is strongly antifeminist, not to say misogynous. Male professors love female graduate students who pay them homage, but dislike female colleagues, especially if they are brighter than themselves. Even the female graduate student must be careful to appear bright enough to appreciate the subtleties and witticisms of her professors, but never to show any signs of outshining them. (This applies to all students, but even more to women.) The best thing that the unmarried female student can do is to become the mistress or wife of a professor, but then to drop any pretense of real academic competition with him. In most cases "nepotism" (in effect, antifeminist) rules will prevent her from doing so anyway. Many universities do not hire both husband and wife, at least not in the same department. In practice, it means the wife gets no job, or one that is clearly inferior in status to that of her husband. And when he changes jobs, she has to follow him, almost never the other way around.

If the student follows a few simple rules of conduct, his chances of survival through graduate school will be enhanced:

1) In seminars, cocktail parties, and similar occasions where groups of students meet with professors, ruthlessly repress any temptation to remain silent. Even if what you say is stupid, there is still the possibility of its appearing profound.

2) Even though all fellow students in your class are your competitors, refrain from criticizing them in front of a professor, because this behavior is almost sure to boomerang against you and to make you extremely unpopular. Try if you can to have the professor criticize your rival. This will be much more effective anyway.

3) Ask your professor penetrating questions, preferably based on books not on the reading list, but make sure that he knows the answer before you ask. Always resist the temptation to expose your professor's ignorance, especially in front of fellow students.

4) By all means, engage your professors in friendly arguments, but always leave them the last word. Try to gauge accurately how far you can push the argument so as to appear at your brightest and enhance the professor's final triumph.

5) Learn the jargon quickly, use it abundantly but accurately, and drop names of authors so as to seem well-read. But be careful whom you quote, and make sure that you know your professor's opinion of whomever you quote. If you do not know his opinion, ask him, but make sure that he has at least heard of the author.

6) Choose your professors with the greatest care, espe-

cially your major one who may later become your thesis adviser. More specifically:

a) Avoid cantankerous isolates, unless they hold positions of exceptional eminence and power, which is seldom the case. Even then, be prepared to be rebuffed.

b) Try to take at least one seminar from most senior professors, whether you are interested in the subject matter or not. But make sure that you know their factional alignments and their relative intellectual position. Until such time as you do, only mention your professors to their colleagues in the most neutral terms.

c) Among your professors, choose as your major one the man who combines the qualities of power in the department and lenience toward students. If he also happens to specialize in an area of interest to you, you are really in luck.

d) As a corollary of the foregoing, choose your area of specialization according to your professors, *not* your professors according to your intellectual interests.

e) Avoid the all-too-successful and popular professor because the chances are that you will seldom see him, and because, if he has too many students, his ability to be of use to you will be diluted, and the competition within his coterie of clients will be intense. However, if you feel confident that you can outshine your competitors, then attach yourself to the star anyway.

f) Cultivate the attitudes, norms, values, and mannerisms associated with your chosen discipline, but do it with *finesse.* Uncritical agreement, slavish imitation, and blatant sycophancy will stamp you as a dull, mediocre chap. For example, share the political liberalism of your professors, but disagree on points of detail. Remember that disagreement is itself one of the norms of academia. Indeed, most scholarly reputations are made disagreeing with the right colleagues at the right time. Flatter your professors, but never in direct, clumsy fashion. E.g., never say: "Hey, professor, that was a good article you wrote in the Micronesian Journal of Politics." Rather, say something like: "Why don't you write a rejoinder to X and put him in his place?" or "Y really made an ass of himself in his review of your book."

7) Cultivate departmental secretaries. Unless some professor hit on the idea before you, you may find it rewarding to take them to dinner and bed, but be discreet about it. Secretaries are often the best informed persons about departmental affairs—amorous, political, and scholarly. They can even wield considerable influence over department chairmen and other powerful figures. Never presume to be of higher status than they are. Remember that for your professors, secretaries are far less dispensable than you are. Consequently, treat them with puntilious courtesy. Who knows? One of them may even type your thesis some day.

8) Accept offers of research or teaching assistantships from your professors, even if they do not seem intrinsically attractive. Remember that a good letter of recommendation from a senior professor when you seek out your first full-time job is worth a couple of hundred hours of slave labor. And if it makes you feel better, call it good experience.

Once you get your Ph.D., the lean years of apprenticeship are over. You have been admitted into the professional priesthood, and you have acquired the privilege of initiating your own novices. By now, you should have "internalized" the norms of your profession and made them your own. You should feel quite comfortable in academe.

⋘ 4 ⋘

Career Strategies

Having spent considerable time, effort, and money on the acquisition of a Ph.D., the young academic now faces the problem of maximizing returns, material and others, on his investment. He is now assured a genteel existence with a comfortable income, abundant leisure, and relative freedom from the insecurities of unemployment, illness, and old age. But, depending on how he plays his cards, he may sink into the oblivion and obscurity of a third-rate college as a mere teacher of undergraduates, or he may rise to the lofty eminence of the professional elite, enjoy the luxuries of life, become a member of the international jet set, and hover around the corridors of power.

We shall confine ourselves here to careers within academia proper—on the staffs of universities and colleges—omitting para-academic employment in foundations, public and private research corporations, and the like. Within academia, three main paths are open which we may provisionally call administration, research, and teaching. These three labels are somewhat misleading because they suggest mutually exclusive activities, and because they imply that one who chooses the "teaching" path spends most of his time in the classroom. Perhaps it would be more accurate to refer to the "teachers" as the "mainstream." Let us turn to this category first, as it includes at least eighty per cent of all academics.

The mainstream consists of those people who hold a regular, graded appointment in a teaching department of a university or college—i.e., the instructors, lecturers, assistant professors, associate professors, and full professors of zoology, romance languages, psychology, and so on. While such appointments almost invariably involve some teaching, professors are also expected to do research and to serve on committees and other administrative bodies. In fact, the more successful professors do very little teaching, but nevertheless, their posts are defined as teaching ones; the backbone of the university's structure is organized around teaching departments.

A mainstream post offers more security of tenure than the other two categories, and the status that attaches to it is unambiguous. Your rank and university place you on a specific rung of the double prestige ladder of academia. Time spent in the junior ranks of lecturer or assistant professor puts you in line for tenure and promotion even if your publication record is mediocre. The detailed tactics of mainstream career advancement deserve a chapter to themselves, but before we turn to them in Chapter Five, let us briefly examine the other two career paths.

The neophyte might think that a research post is the golden road to academic fame, and hence will frequently let himself be lured by a seemingly attractive job in a research organization associated with a university. Frequently these jobs are doubly alluring because they involve no teaching at all, and because the salaries are substantially above that which a beginner could earn in an assistant professorship. The young Ph.D., who by now has thoroughly internalized the norm that teaching is to be avoided and that research is all that counts, jumps at such opportunities to put his dreams into practice. Little does he appreciate the shortcomings of his career choice.

First, the salary differential is more apparent than real. Mainstream jobs are usually for nine months and can easily be supplemented by summer teaching or research. Research posts, on the other hand are usually for eleven or twelve months. In most cases, the misleading differential disappears if one computes the monthly figure by dividing teaching salaries into nine rather than twelve.

Second, research jobs are frequently supported by some research grant which runs for a limited number of years, often no more than five years. Thus, they lack permanence and security.

Third, the research conducted in those institutes is frequently designed and even partially executed by others, so the individual loses much independence of action. The research director may be able to determine research policy, but he is typically so busy running his institute that he has no time to do much actual research himself and is in fact an administrator of research funds and personnel. His subordinates are interdependent parts of a team, not autonomous intellectuals free to pursue their own fancies.

Fourth, it follows from the above that the individual also loses his freedom to publish what and when he wants. Since the research is typically communal, so is most published work, and, much as in the proverbial ship convoy, the speed of the team is determined by its slowest member. This means that material for publication is often delayed (if it ever comes out at all), and at early career stages this can be quite crippling.

Fifth, research jobs do not have any well-defined status in the academic hierarchy. They do not clearly convey to a prospective employer reading a candidate's *vita* where the candidate ought to fit in the mainstream ranking system. This in turn means that if a person seeks to enter the mainstream from a research post, his placement will be almost solely determined by his publications. It also means that he will frequently have to take a salary cut.

Finally, a research position frequently isolates you from most colleagues in your discipline, and hence puts you outside the hottest circuits of influence in the job market.

And so it follows that research jobs are often more limiting than teaching jobs in terms of what research you can do, that they tend to delay rather than hasten publication, and that, being ephemeral, they force most people back into the mainstream at a later stage. In the vast majority of cases, the point of entry into that mainstream is lower than if the person had started a few years earlier as an assistant professor. Only a highly prolific printed output can ward off that fate, and the publication outlook as we have seen is frequently worse than in a teaching post. The few exceptions to the rule are people with the push and ability to succeed in spite of their mistakes. Regular academic departments at major universities are the safest havens and offer the best prospects of advancement in academia.

There remains to consider the path of college or university administration. Until well into the 20th century, American colleges and universities had a fairly simple table of organization. They had a president and board of trustees, half a dozen deans with their secretaries, and a chairman for each department. Frequently the most senior member of the department was the permanent chairman of it. Deanships were offered to professors who had outlived their usefulness as productive scholars but who were still a few years short of retirement age, and had shown a flair for not antagonizing their colleagues and not rocking the boat. And presidents achieved their position by dressing in respectable Ivy League suits, by making tolerable after-dinner speeches at alumni functions, by expressing conservative political views to their boards of trustees and liberal ones to their faculty, and by being able to make the wealthy disgorge part of their ill-acquired gains for the construction of buildings named after them.

These idyllic days are over. Academic administration has become a specialty in its own right: college bureaucracies assume more and more imposing proportions; and the links between academic bureaucrats and their teaching colleagues become increasingly tenuous. Today we have vice-presidents, provosts, associate deans, assistant deans, administrative assistants, executive secretaries, assistant chairmen, deputy provosts, and so on, not to mention armies of typists caressing the keys of their electric machines, miniskirted filing clerks brushing their slender hips along rows of metal cabinets, and receptionists whispering seductively over the telephone.

Department chairmen are hybrids between teaching staff and administrators. Traditionally, their position was fairly permanent and wielded more authority than is the case now. The more mediocre a college, the more the old pattern of autocratic and permanent chairmen persists, and the more a department headship is still regarded as a desirable job. Professionally weak departments make for strong chairmen, and vice versa. At first-rate universities, however, chairmen have lost virtually all power, and the material rewards are not commensurate with the load of trivial, uninteresting tasks that go with the job. Like other administrators, chairmen are on year-round jobs, and, apart from one or two extra months' salary and bigger offices, get no advantages over other senior colleagues. The main function of a modern chairman is to serve as an intermediary and a negotiator between his staff and the dean. Most of all, he must fight for promotions and salary raises, for a bigger budget, and for new appointments. While the old-style department head was a kind of foreman over his colleagues, the new-style chairman is more like a shop steward.

At major institutions, chairmanships are so unattractive that they are regarded as a chore which full professors are morally obliged to assume in rotation for a period of two to five years on the average. Sometimes they even have to be filled by associate professors for lack of full professors willing to assume the self-defeating task of keeping their colleagues happy and of getting A promoted without antagonizing B. To make the job less onerous, executive secretaries and assistant chairmen take care of the more routine tasks, and the important decisions are taken in most cases by formal committees or by an informal oligarchy of full professors, rather than by the chairman himself.

Thus the chairman's main job is to be a perpetual mendicant to the dean on behalf of his department, and to sign a voluminous correspondence. The chairman has the worse of both worlds: he assumes administrative responsibilities without effective power, and loses the leisure and independence of the ordinary professor.

If one wants to become an administrator, then one might as well make a clean break with the mainstream and become a dean. Deans used to be promoted (some might say "demoted") from the ranks of full professors, especially those who had proven themselves in departmental chairmanships. A deanship was a decorous solution to intellectual senescence, a process which in the physical sciences and mathematics begins in one's thirties, and in the humanities and social sciences not all that much later.

Today, the trend is increasingly for the administrative path to bifurcate from the mainstream earlier, and for the two to become more and more tenuously related. The way to a deanship is more and more through an assistant and associate deanship, rather than through a professorship and departmental headship. The fiction that administrators remain academics is still preserved, and most senior administrators retain a nominal affiliation with a teaching department, but a young man can now opt quite early for a distinctly administrative career and work his way up the hierarchy from assistant dean to president.

What, then, are the advantages, if any, of an administrative career? The first one is that intellectual mediocrity is less likely to show up in an administrative job than in a teaching one. Academic administration is probably more cumbersome, dilatory, and inefficient than other bureaucracies, and administrators can easily avoid the charge of incompetence by blaming the system. Indeed much of this inefficiency is due to the facts that the lines of authority are not clear, that professors do not let themselves be pushed around and will sabotage by passive resistance any reform of which they do not approve, and that much of the decision-making is diffused through a slow-moving committee structure.

An administrative career will also appeal to persons who enjoy "working with" (i.e., manipulating) people. Deanships vary greatly in prestige and power depending on the status of those who are manipulated. Thus, deans of students, deans of admissions, and deans of graduate schools have relatively low prestige because they push around mere students. Conversely, the dean of arts and sciences, as the key pusher of the largest bulk of the faculty at a university, is usually top dog among deans, and often the second most powerful person after the president. However, his actual power over staff is severely curtailed by the effective use of resignation threats. Professors have little need for collective bargaining because their individual bargaining is so effective.

Generally, deans and other high-ranking administrators do not enjoy either the power or the prestige commensurate to their official rank in the university hierarchy. The internationally known professor is the prima donna of the university, not the dean who in most cases is a purely local figure. The person who is intrinsically interested in power and administration will thus probably do better if he joins government, a large business corporation, or a foundation. As bureaucracies go, academic ones are fairly low-powered.

The material rewards of university administration are

probably the most tangible ones. The one thing that college bureaucrats can do quite well is to maneuvre themselves into salaries that their generally modest intellectual endowment could not earn them in mainstream jobs. They are also remarkably successful in arrogating to themselves such fringe benefits as plentiful office space and reserved parking spots. The Nobel Prize winner in physics may have to spend fifteen minutes every morning hunting for a place to leave his VW, but the associate dean of men will have his reserved parking on the doorstep of his office. All these material advantages, however, are purchased at the cost of considerable loss in leisure compared to the mainstream academic who works some eight months a year.

In conclusion, the academic administrator is neither fish nor fowl. The person with a bureaucratic vocation can do better outside universities and colleges, and the person with an academic vocation can do better in the mainstream if he is any good. Only at mediocre universities (characterized by weak faculties and tyrannical administrations) is it really worthwhile to become a campus bureaucrat. But then who wants to be at a mediocre university?

A few words remain to be said about two types of academics: the "locals" and the "cosmopolites."[1] We have seen that academics belong to two communities of scholars—the geographically dispersed members of their discipline, and the localized members of their university or college. Those to whom the first group is most important are the cosmopolites, while the locals focus their life and aspirations on their campus. Some professors are active in

[1]The terms were first used by Alvin W. Gouldner, one of those rare, civilized sociologists who know how to write.

both their home campus and in their professional association, but most of them can be fairly readily classified as belonging to one of the two categories. Locals have deeper roots in the campus and town; they serve on a lot of university committees; they belong to the Faculty Club; they give free talks to church and business groups; they join various voluntary associations in town; they do not travel much; they receive few outside offers and therefore show great loyalty to their institution and change jobs infrequently; they publish little; they get involved in university and municipal or state politics; and a few of the more successful ones finish their careers as deans or provosts. To a layman, locals may look like the big wheels at their universities, and indeed much of the local decision-making is in their hands because the cosmopolites could not care less who becomes head librarian or whether the Faculty Club should organize bridge tournaments. But locals, by definition, are not big-league academics.

Cosmopolites, on the other hand, travel a lot to conferences and professional meetings; avoid time-consuming committee assignments and other chores at their university; publish as much and teach as little as they can; strike few local roots and are prepared to pull them up on a fortnight's notice; and play politics in their professional association where, if successful, they may end up elected president. Cosmopolites tend to be contemptuous of locals, and the locals envious of cosmopolites. The successful cosmopolite gets plenty of job offers, and consequently can extract more from his home university than can locals through long years of devoted service.

It might be supposed that only people of exceptional ability become successful cosmopolites, but this is far from true. While getting known through one's published work certainly *is* a way of reaching the top of one's profession and of acquiring an international reputation, these aims can also be achieved by studiously attending conventions, cultivating the influentials, editing and reviewing the works of others, infiltrating the key committees of one's association, canvassing for elective office, agitating for popular causes, and otherwise enhancing one's visibility and audibility wherever colleagues meet. It is doubtful that successful cosmopolites are of much greater intellectual caliber than successful locals. Cosmopolites simply have a different life style and enjoy higher prestige. The more able academics are generally attracted by the cosmopolitan style, but they are not necessarily successful in association politics. Conversely, mediocrity gives one no assurance of success as a local, and some prominent locals are very able chaps who might have made good as cosmopolites.

The great superiority of the cosmopolites over the locals is that the former nearly always win hands down over the latter in competing for the rewards of a given university. The great irony of academia is that faithful locals are scarcely ever rewarded for their hard work; they do not have the option of leaving their university, and hence they are taken for granted and are passed over in promotion and salary raises. The cosmopolite, by threatening to leave and thus expressing his lack of loyalty to his university, can in fact get much more out of it than the local. Whether he stays or leaves, the cosmopolite ends up ahead, simply because he has options. By contrast, the local's only chance of success is an appointment to a high administrative post. To the naïve dismay of locals, cosmopolites almost always beat them on their own home grounds.

It follows from the above, then, that the sensible academic will want to enter the mainstream through an appointment in a teaching department, and that he will follow a cosmopolitan strategy of career advancement. Let us now see in greater detail how he must play that game.

»» 5 ««

The Fat Years: Salary, Tenure, and Promotions

The cardinal principle of career advancement is: When in doubt, move. In order to move up fast in rank and salary you must either move out in space or threaten to do so. The person who is unable to leave his university because he fell in love with the locale, or because his wife wants to stay close to her parents, or because he does not get any outside offers, must inevitably fall behind his leap-frogging colleagues. The fewer your roots, the more unimpeded your race to the top. Each year, between late June and early September, tens of thousands of academics pack up and crisscross the North American continent in an apparently random migration.

The collective impression of meaninglessness given by these migrations can in fact be broken down into thousands of highly sensible individual decisions. For the academic world as a whole, for the various universities and colleges, and for the students, professional seminomadism not only serves no useful purpose: it is in fact positively wasteful and harmful. But for the professors it is enormously profitable.

Let us first try to understand the main features and determinants of this complex annual relocation. Sociologists refer to mobility in space as horizontal, and to mobility in status as vertical. The latter can be either up or down. In academia, vertical mobility takes place in reference to a double status system: academic rank and prestige of university.

The academic market place is a vast system in which the top universities have their pick of topnotch men in every field. (The well-known boast of Harvard is that when it tries to fill a post it always appoints the best man and usually finds that the person is already on its staff.) There is of course a certain amount of competition between Harvard and Berkeley, or between Columbia and Chicago, or between Yale and Princeton, but the top schools are definitely in a buyer's market. They have fewer posts than there are candidates who would be delighted to jump at the opportunity to join their staffs. But below the very top, universities have to face a seller's market and to compete fiercely with each other for the best possible staff—i.e., for people whose established individual prestige is likely to enhance the prestige of the hiring institution and department. Although appointments are officially confirmed by the board of trustees and the president, the bargaining parties in the transactions are in the first instance the candidate and the hiring department. The dean of the faculty in question in most cases has to approve the rank and salary offered, but at respectable universities he seldom chooses the candidates.

Since the overwhelming majority of universities and

colleges are by definition not the top ones, the market as a whole may be described as a seller's, with intense competition between buyers. Colleges and universities have expanded faster then they have produced Ph.D.'s, and, in addition, teaching loads have gone steadily down. Consequently, the demand for qualified teachers outstrips the supply by an ever-widening margin. So far, the universities and colleges have agreed on practically nothing to restrict their cut-throat competition for staff except on an April closing date for the hunting season, and even that is frequently violated.

The individual academic will try to maximize his status —that is, to get as high a rank (and salary) as he can at the best possible university. In practice, his decision may be contaminated by other factors such as climate, proximity to relatives, and so on, but rank and institutional prestige are the two most powerful determinants of horizontal moves. The relationship between vertical and horizontal moves is quite complex, but basically, horizontal moves can be determined by four types of vertical moves:

1) A move up in both academic rank and institutional prestige. These are undoubtedly the best ones, but they are not very common.

2) A move up in institutional prestige but without promotion in rank.

3) A promotion in rank to an equal-status institution.

4) A promotion in rank to a lower-status institution.

The third type of move is probably the most common, followed in descending order by types Four, Two, and One. Type Four moves are really downward in spite of the promotion in rank. This is what happens to assistant professors at prestigious institutions if they do not publish enough. After five or six years, they are denied tenure and forced to go because of the "up or out" rule. Either you get promoted to associate professor with tenure or you must leave, almost invariably to a lower-status institution. In anticipation of that fate, many assistant professors trade their institutional prestige for the best possible deal at a lower-status university and move before they are forced to do so. But whether forced or not, such moves are nearly always irreversible in terms of institutional prestige.

The fiercest competition for staff is between institutions of approximately equal status. Until recently, a university would only raid campuses of equal or slightly higher status than itself and would mostly get downwardly mobile staff from higher-status institutions. Even so, if the status difference between the two universities was too great, the lower-status campus would have wasted its time trying to raid its betters, and thus the competition for staff was confined to fairly narrow limits within the total status spectrum. Apache Valley Community College would never have the audacity of trying to raid Princeton or Michigan. Of late, however, as competition has become increasingly fierce, universities are beginning to raid institutions of somewhat lower rank than themselves and stealing their stars. Thus the raiding range has become wider than it used to be, and Type One moves are somewhat more frequent than before. The days when the Ivy League schools or the Big Ten would only steal each other's staff are gone. Still, institutions of widely different status do not compete with each other.

It should also be noted that rates of mobility, both horizontal and vertical, are greatest in the early part of a person's career, and decline thereafter. Assistant professors are highly mobile, associate professors less so, and professors least. There are three reasons for this. The first one is that the closer you are to the top, the less room you have to move up. The second reason is that the higher your rank and your price tag, the smaller the range of institutions that can afford you and also want you. By the time you are a full professor at a respectable university, you must be a well-known quantity, in fact a star, to be attractive to higher-status universities, and the offers you get tend to be from lower-status institutions trying to make up for their lack of prestige by offering you low teaching loads and high salaries. Finally, mobility declines after a few years because most academics tend to find their level in the hierarchy of universities and to stay there, unless they do something extraordinarily opprobrious or meritorious.

Since much of the academic migration takes place between institutions of approximately equal status, why could it not be reduced to a fraction of its present proportions? More specifically, why should every university have to lose year after year a substantial proportion of its best staff, only to be forced to snatch from its competitors no more qualified professors at higher prices than it was willing to pay the people who left?

There are two main ways in which a university could substantially reduce this migratory movement. One would be to enter into collective agreements restricting competition such as are effectively used by business firms. But it is obvious why universities do no such thing. Universities are run by and for professors, and since the present system is so advantageous to most academics, the incentive to change it is nil. The universities as institutions, the students, and the taxpayers suffer from academic nomadism, but the nomads prosper and, in between treks, they run the campuses. In fact, it is quite common for professors at conferences to be recruiting for their own university while at the same time be soliciting offers from colleagues on similar recruiting jaunts. Academics create in effect the demand for their own services, restrict the supply by keeping their crops of Ph.D.'s small, and thus successfully raid the public and corporate purses that support the entire operation.

The second way of reducing migration is, of course, for the home university to make a counteroffer in order to keep a person. This is quite commonly done, and does, no doubt, reduce the migration to onehalf or less of what it would otherwise be. But there are intrinsic limitations to the effectiveness of this device. In the first place, a person always looks better from the outside than he does from the inside. It is one thing to create an impression of brilliance and agreeableness in the course of a few hours of convivial interviews over martinis, but quite another to sustain that impression over years of close contact with your home colleagues. Thus, a dean may, often rightly, decide that a man is not worth the rank and salary he is offered elsewhere, and let him go by making a counteroffer which is deliberately low enough to be turned down. Alternatively, a man's senior colleagues in a department may be glad to be rid of him because of his cantankerous disposition, theoretical orientation, embarrassing brightness, or some other reason. In short, there is often no attempt at keeping a man, or the attempt is so perfunctory that it fails, as it is intended to do.

In addition, there is an important factor of "status inertia" within each department. A person's worth tends to be pegged at the level of his entry point into a department. He assumes a definite place in the pecking order, and, thereafter, any promotion or rapid salary raise which would drastically disturb that pecking order will be resisted by his colleagues. Once a man has entered a department at a given level, any progress at a rate faster than the departmental average will be seen as disturbing the established hierarchy. (Oddly, the reverse is also true. A colleague whose progress is much slower than average, e.g., an assistant professor in his fifties, is also a source of acute embarrassment.) It is much easier, on the other hand, to accept a young newcomer in a high position because this involves no change in the pecking order other than inserting the newcomer into it at a mutually agreed upon place.

The implications of status inertia for horizontal mobility are clear. It is very difficult to move upward fast by staying at the same place. And since the quickest avenue of success is publication, a high rate of productivity means a frequent encounter with the moving van.

Related to the previous factor is the fact that many young Ph.D.'s begin their careers at the "wrong" level, and must change jobs to find a better fit. Only the most prestigious universities can afford to underpay productive scholars without losing them. Mediocre universities with a lot of dead wood in the senior ranks do not really try to keep bright young men even if they could afford to do so. If you are either too bright or too dull for the university at which you are located, life is made very unpleasant for you. In the former case, you will be the butt of envy and be accused of arrogance; and in the latter you will be constantly humiliated. Fortunately, outside offers will allow you to find your own level. Thus, individual mobility insures a certain constancy of quality at given universities.

In short, then, even with counteroffers, mobility is endemic in the system. The problem now is how to make the most of it. Let us begin with the young man who has just received his Ph.D. The choice of a first academic job is extremely crucial, and unfortunately this is the stage of one's career where one is most completely dependent on the good grace of others, especially one's major professors in graduate school.

At that stage, unless he has already published, a candidate is evaluated on two things: the quality of his Ph.D., as judged by the prestige of the department which conferred it, and the quality of his letters of recommendations, depending on how glowing they are and how influential their writers are. Thus a Ph.D. from one of the "top ten" departments and an assessment as "one of the best three or four students I have ever had" by a national figure gives him a virtual assurance of a good first job at a prestige university. The same Ph.D. from the same university but with a lukewarm recommendation as a "sound, competent student" downgrades the candidate to a not-so-good university or college. The best jobs are often obtained informally through verbal recommendations at scholarly meetings. As to the employment columns of trade journals and the placement services at meetings, they are generally last resorts for the downwardly mobile and for Ph.D.'s from second-rate universities.

To the extent that a young Ph.D. has some choice of likely jobs and does not feel obligated to accept the one job that his major professor lined up for him, there are three main factors which should determine his decision:

1) The teaching load should be as low as possible, cer-

tainly not over nine hours, and preferably not over six. This is probably the key condition, because your entire career depends on how much time you have to do research and publish during your first five post-doctoral years.

2) Salary is a somewhat less important consideration and should not be computed on the basis of the gross annual figure, but prorated on the basis of the length and amount of work expected of you. Thus a $9,000 teaching job for eight months of work a year is better than an $11,000 year-round research job. Or $8,500 for a six-hour teaching load is better than $10,000 for a nine-hour load.

3) The prestige of the institution is important but with several caveats and reservations. There is of course a limit below which you should not go if you can possibly help it, but the *most* prestigious institutions have their pitfalls. First, it is important not to confuse social prestige and academic prestige. For example, the elite liberal arts colleges tend to be undesirable because they are altogether outside big-league academia, are often geographically isolated, do not have graduate students, lack adequate library and laboratory facilities, and expect you to take undergraduate teaching seriously. Second, the temptation to hang on at the university that granted you a Ph.D. must be resisted at all costs, for the reason of status inertia mentioned earlier. At your *alma mater* you will always be a student, unless you let a decade elapse, by which time most of your former professors will have retired, died, or left the university. Try to come back later, in a tenure job, but, meanwhile, resolutely cut the umbilical cord. Otherwise, you will progress very slowly, and may have to leave anyway after a few years if you are not granted tenure.

Thirdly, the very-high-status universities are characterized by intense competition among assistant professors, powerful publication pressures, low probability of getting promoted to a tenure rank after five or six years of anxious expectation, slow promotion even if you make the grade, and mediocre salaries and fairly high teaching loads in the lower ranks. As a junior academic, the price you have to pay for institutional prestige is rather high. Prestige universities are best entered at the top level or at least at the associate professor level, if at all.

Finally, you have to be wary of accepting "service" jobs outside the department of your own discipline, no matter how alluring the university might be. Thus, for example, for a psychologist to take up a position in a school of education, or an economist in a business school, or a sociologist in a medical school can turn out to be a professional blind alley even though it is at Teacher's College, Columbia, or at the Harvard Business School, or at the Johns Hopkins Medical School.

All things considered, the ideal school for the professionally ambitious young scholar is the large state or private university just below the top-ten level, with adequate research facilities and low teaching loads. The place has to be good enough to offer the opportunities and contacts for career advancement, yet not so notable that the assistant professor has little if any bargaining power. Most Big Ten universities, for example, satisfy these conditions, except perhaps Chicago and Michigan which are a little too prestigious. Most assistant professors who start off at the very top end will end up getting tenure appointments one rung below that anyway, and their brief sojourn in the lofty pinnacles of academe typically costs them a two or three years' delay in promotion and quite a few thousand dollars compared to what they might have gotten in a place where they would have had some bargaining power. At the very top, assistant professors are interchangeable nonentities hired to teach undergraduate courses so that their world-famous seniors can spend most of their time on leave in Washington, Oxford, or Karachi.

Assuming that your Ph.D. has landed you a good job with a low teaching load at a respectable university, you must now fight your way to the top of your profession in terms of rank, salary, and tenure. If you play your cards right and if you publish what is regarded as the appropriate quota in your discipline, you should be a full professor within seven to ten years of getting your doctorate. In other words, you should spend no more than four to five years in each of the two ranks of assistant and associate professor.

Tenure used to be important when professors were not in as good a bargaining position as now, but now it is rapidly losing its significance, except as a protection for political radicals. Since it is clearly in your interest to change jobs, and since your university is chronically short of staff, tenure becomes an irrelevance. Nevertheless many universities still take it seriously. In the vast majority of cases, tenure comes with appointment or promotion to an associate professorship. Assistant professors are almost always appointed for a term of three to five years, usually renewable once. Thereafter, they are either promoted and given tenure, or asked to find themselves another job. A few universities do not grant tenure with any first appointment even of full professors, but they are the exception.

Whatever significance tenure still has, it no longer lies in the privilege of hanging on to a job until you are senile.

Rather, the meaning of tenure is the evaluation procedure which it entails after no more than six years in an assistant professorship. (The six-year limit for the "up or out" decision is a convention agitated for by the American Association of University Professors, and generally adhered to by universities for fear of censure.) In short, if a man cares to stay where he is, he must within a few years convince his senior colleagues that he is worth promoting and keeping permanently. Being linked with promotion to an associate professorship, this decision is in fact the most decisive jump in a man's career, even though tenure as such is of little practical significance.

A few institutions, mostly pretentious little liberal arts colleges, still hold to a quaintly anachronistic conception of tenure, namely that tenure is granted to the man who has proven his "loyalty" (whatever that means) to the institution. At most schools, however, tenure has no such sentimental undertones; it is simply the most inconsequential part of a package deal which also involves promotion and a salary raise.

University policies in respect to salary vary widely. Some schools have overlapping salary scales between ranks so that an assistant professor may earn more than an associate professor or an associate more than a full professor. Other institutions do not. On some campuses salaries are supposed to be strictly confidential while at others, notably at many state universities, they are published yearly. Confidential salaries always put the staff at a considerable disadvantage, and one might think that academics would have the sense to exchange that information for their mutual benefit in haggling for raises, but at most snob schools, this conduct is regarded as ungentlemanly, much as going on strike and other forms of unseemly behavior characteristic of the laboring classes. In some cases, salary scales provide for automatic annual increments, while in others every raise has to be justified on the basis of "merit."

Almost invariably, however, the biggest raises are obtained either by changing jobs or by threatening to do so. Once established, this system becomes self-reenforcing. Most deans dispose of a fixed sum for yearly salary increments. They first have to dig into it to make counteroffers to members of their staff who are in a good bargaining position. The remainder goes to automatic or "merit" increments. But in most cases, "merit" increases tend to go to the least meritorious. After the productive members of the department have received their negotiated raises, the rest of the pie is distributed to the unproductive members who do not get outside offers. Thus, "merit" increases are used mostly for purposes of salary equalization within ranks, according to a rationale of "equity" and seniority. The least productive members tend to get "merit" increases; the productive ones get negotiated counteroffers.

Unless a productive scholar is willing to pay the price of chronic underpayment, he cannot escape from an aggressive and "ungentlemanly" tactic of haggling on the basis of outside offers. If he does not play the game, his salary becomes aligned with that of his most undistinguished colleagues and quickly falls behind that of his more aggressive juniors. Outside offers create a gap between the productive staff and the dead wood; and the principle of "equity" makes use of "merit" increases to bridge that gap. Aggressiveness is the only option for those who are in a good bargaining position.

The same applies to promotions. The person who modestly waits until his senior colleagues recognize his merits will essentially be promoted in order of seniority if at all. With outside offers, the process can be accelerated by at least one hundred per cent.

This leads us to the academic game par excellence, the outside offer. The game is extremely profitable, but it requires considerable finesse; any dean worth his salt has become at least as adept a player as an inexperienced assistant professor. Let us look at the game first from the dean's perspective. His problem is to satiate unlimited demands with limited funds. Or, more precisely, he must try to retain as many of his best staff as he can, and hire quite a few new ones besides, without going broke. Thus, a dean must first ask the person's department head and senior colleagues whether they are very keen to retain the person, and, upon receiving an affirmative answer, he must make an accurate assessment of the minimum rank and salary for which the scholar will stay put. This involves solving a complex equation with many unknowns, but the basic calculation takes the outside offer as the starting point and subtracts from or adds to it.

If the offer involves a double upward jump in terms of both institutional prestige, and rank and salary, the dean has little hope of retaining the person. He will rarely offer *more* money than the outside school because this would be an admission that the dean's own university has lower status, and most deans have a slightly inflated notion of their own university's prestige. Thus, he will be content with matching the rank and salary of the offer and wish the person all the best if he decides to leave, as indeed he should.

If the offer comes from a school of distinctly lower

status, the dean will not as a rule consider it serious and will not make a counteroffer. He banks on the probability that the higher rank and salary are not sufficient compensation for the loss in institutional prestige, and he regards it as below his university's dignity to compete downward. At best, he may offer the person a small salary raise if he feels that he otherwise deserves it, but if he is of a nasty disposition he will smile and say, "Sorry, no dice."

The really difficult calculations involve cases where the two schools are of approximately equal status. There the dean's mind will work somewhat as follows: University of X offers, say, $15,000 without moving expenses. It will cost Y some $800 to get down there with his three children and impedimenta; Y will probably lose $1,000 on the sale of his house (assuming that he was foolish enough to buy one before getting tenure); the cost of living in X is about three per cent higher than here; X offers five per cent less in retirement benefits; I know that Y, an avid skier, likes his present location and that is worth at least $300 a year to him; on the other hand the climate is better in X so that cancels out the previous item. Answer: $12,000 is the break-even point. Y now makes $11,500. If I only offer him $12,000, he will feel offended and might leave out of spite. I shall play it safe and offer him $12,500—about a ten per cent increment— and, if he still squawks, I will go up to $13,000 and make him feel like going out with his wife to celebrate.

Should the offer also involve a promotion, as it frequently does, the calculation becomes more complex yet. The dean must see if he can offer the salary raise without the promotion, he must assess how much value Y puts on the rank as such, and how much Y's colleagues would resent his promotion and the resulting change in the pecking order. Finally he must try to anticipate how many of Y's colleagues are in a position actively to push for promotion in order to reestablish a situation close to the *status quo ante* in the said pecking order.

The game is equally complex from the professor's point of view, and miscalculations can be so costly to his self-esteem that he has no graceful option but to make an unwanted move. That is the greatest hazard in the game. Happily, this outcome can be avoided by observing a few simple rules:

1) Try to assess correctly your value to your department. The common mistake is, of course, to overrate yourself, and nothing is more embarrassing than having your department chairman congratulate you warmly when you break the good news to him, and make no hint of any other response. Your best option then is to try to hide your blush as you file past the secretaries in the front office, swallow your pride, and play it more carefully next time.

2) Assess correctly the relative status of your university and the one that makes the offer. A common failing here is that a person, especially a beginner at the game, feels so flattered by the offer that he will inflate the prestige of the school concerned so as to increase further the value of the offer. Remember that the dean will have a bias in the other direction, and that the gap between the two assessments may be so wide as to make negotiations impossible.

3) *Never* state your terms for staying. This commits you to a position from which you cannot gracefully withdraw, and it antagonizes deans who regard this behavior as impertinence unless it emanates from a very senior man. Furthermore, it does not get you anywhere. A common

reaction to this is to say: Let the arrogant bloke go.

4) Do not bluff, because the chances are that your bluff will be called. Effective bargaining presupposes that the offer is attractive enough to you that you *might* leave. But you gain nothing by stating that you want to leave. On the contrary, express a preference for staying. It is already implied in the negotiation process itself that you might leave, and stating it merely antagonizes your chairman and your dean who do not like to feel *forced* into a course of action.

5) Do not jeopardize your chances of getting substantial gains for the sake of a momentary satisfaction of your vanity or spite. Make no deprecating remarks about your present department as this will turn your colleagues against you; and do not brag about your offers, especially not before they become "firm"—i.e., before you get a letter stating the precise terms thereof.

6) Let your department chairman do the talking to the dean unless you have good reasons to suspect that he might not represent your interests well. One of the main conditions for successful bargaining is to be on good terms with your chairman. If your chairman is hostile to you, he can easily steer the negotiations in such a way as to maneuver you out of the department.

7) Only make use of strong offers, and remember that the game cannot be played too often. In fact, it should be used no more often than every two years. A more frequent use of outside offers reduces the effectiveness of the game and taxes the patience of the chairman and the dean.

8) Do not hesitate to leave if the counteroffer is distinctly inferior to the offer, especially if the promotion is not matched, but do not move too often. Again, every other

year is about the maximum. More frequent moves look bad on a *vita* and give one a reputation for shiftlessness, especially if the moves are not clearly upward ones in terms of rank, university prestige, or both. Try to avoid moves without promotions unless the new university is of clearly superior status to the one you leave.

The beginner might well ask how one gets offers. Offers can be either solicited or unsolicited. Early in one's career they have to be solicited by canvassing one's old professors and classmates in graduate school. Another source of offers are hand-me-downs from better established colleagues who, in declining offers, drop your name as a likely "movable." Later, when you get well established, offers are mostly unsolicited and a nuisance. Every time you get a "feeler" you must write a polite "thanks but no thanks" letter.

The process of getting a "firm" offer is itself protracted and requires some skill. Offers begin as "feelers," all the way from a casual question at a convention to a formal letter stating that Department X is expanding and planning great things, and would you be interested in hearing more about it? Many feelers get no further, and you should always refrain from bragging about them. The next step is usually a long-distance telephone call suggesting a visit to the campus, all expenses paid and no obligation of course. Then comes the visit with its round of formal and informal interviews, its ritualistic seminars and cocktail parties, its exchanges of pleasantries, and its awkward private sessions with deans and department heads.

Occasionally, if you have created a bad impression, nothing comes of the visit, but in most cases the next step is a formal offer in writing often preceded by a telephone call to announce it and followed by another one asking you to make up your mind. You usually have to write a letter stalling for time in order to have time to negotiate at home. "I have to talk it over with my wife" is always a good gambit in American society. "It is a difficult decision and I find your offer very attractive" is another possibility. Or else you might suggest that you would like to come but that the salary is not high enough.

From start to finish, the process usually takes a minimum of three weeks and a maximum of six weeks. The cost to the "offering" university is your round-trip plus many man-hours of professorial time. The cost to your home university is whatever it has to give you to keep you. The cost to you is two or three days for travel and interviews and a little mental unsettlement, but assuming that you only make $1,000 salary increment out of it, that still means $300 to $500 per day invested in the interview routine.

The height of the hunting season is from January through March, but as competition gets keener, the season is extended further and further back, sometimes as far back as the fall conventions. In fact, the system is now so wide open that raiding is practically continuous, but intensified in the winter months.

Salary and rank are the bread and butter of an academic appointment. The "fringe benefits" are the marmalade. Retirement plan is one of the most important of them. Depending on whether it is contributory or not, or transferable to another university or not, the retirement system can make a difference of up to fifteen per cent either way in the monetary value of an offer. Medical plan, life insurance, sabbatical policy, educational benefits for your children, and moving expense compensation are also appreciable parts of the package. Sabbaticals are actually not as valuable as they appear, because since they are almost invariably on reduced pay, they are scarcely sufficient to travel on. If you stay in residence at your university, you might as well not be on leave at all because you will find it difficult to get away from your normal routine. The thing to do is to find foundation or government support for a leave of absence. This will normally cover all of your regular salary plus travel and research expenses.

Most of these fringe benefits are part of a standard deal which is the same for all members of the teaching staff. Others are more variable. Office space is perhaps the main one of these. Especially at urban universities, the scarcity of office space is acute, and the doubling up of assistant professors is a common practice. An assistant professor should then be wary of accepting an office large enough to be doubled-up, because even if he has it to himself now, he might have to share it later. The safest kind of office to have is 80 to 100 square feet, large enough to turn around in but too small to accommodate more than a single desk and bookcase.

A word remains to be said about personality factors which often have a direct bearing on career progress. Although a great many departments try to maintain a fiction of consensus, nearly all are characterized by competition, conflict, and factionalism. The decision to promote an assistant professor is, at least in the first instance, made by the more senior members of the department, or by the chairman in consultation with them. The case then often goes to a faculty-wide committee of elected members of the tenured staff, who make recommendations to the dean of the faculty. In theory, a man often has a right to appeal against a negative decision of his chairman and senior colleagues, but, in fact, if he bucks his department, the cards are stacked heavily against him, unless he has an exceptionally strong case.

There are two necessary and sufficient conditions under which your colleagues will recommend you for tenure and promotion. The first is that you have published enough to make a case to the College Council, Promotions Committee, or whatever the higher body is called. The second is that you pass the test of "fitting into the department." This is, of course, primarily a personality test. You must appear "constructive"—i.e., you must not stir up the students, criticize past practices, suggest drastic reforms, raise painful questions, or stand on universalistic principles when your colleagues give vent to blatant favoritism.

Most important of all, you must show the degree of humility commensurate with your still modest status, and you must ruthlessly suppress any temptation to prove yourself intellectually superior to your seniors. That is the one thing for which they will never forgive you. (In any case, this is a facile and unworthy exercise, because the processes of senescence and obsolescence insure that assistant professors *are* on the whole considerably brighter and more up to date than full professors.) Try also to be noncommittal about important issues that sharply divide the senior staff; you cannot yet afford to antagonize any important faction.

At departmental meetings, do not talk too much, but do not remain completely silent either, otherwise you will be eclipsed by your more aggressive rivals and passed over in promotions because of your colorlessness. The best course consists in letting your seniors talk and commit themselves first, especially on controversial issues. Listen carefully to what they say and learn to predict individual positions on key matters. If the issue bitterly splits the department down the middle, do not say anything and abstain on any nonsecret ballots. If the split is between old guard and young Turks, side with the old guard, but do so discreetly. Avoid any blatant sycophancy. Flattery has to be subtle if it is to be effective in academia.

The issues on which you should talk and demonstrate your good sense and constructiveness are the ones that are not too controversial—for example, minor procedural reforms in admission of graduate students, or small changes in curriculum or doctoral examinations. Speak in support of suggestions made by an influential senior, and make a few embellishments of your own to show that you have devoted thought to the subject, but do not advocate any drastic departures from existing procedures because this might appear to cast aspersions against the wisdom of your elders. Thus you will appear to be an eminently sensible young man, mature beyond his years, and very suitable tenure material. All you will have to do is produce your minimum quota of printed matter, and your promotion is assured.

If you are a woman, these considerations hold even more, for then you will not only have to demonstrate your humility as a junior but also stay in your place as a member of the inferior sex. It is bad enough that you should aspire to be an academic instead of getting domesticated and pregnant like most of your kind, so you cannot afford to be aggressive, nor even to seem too bright. If you must appear bright, then let it be in support of an even brighter male colleague. Otherwise, just play the role of the sweet female; smile and be vivacious, but never ironical.

In any case, you will probably have to wait longer for your promotion than your male colleagues, but then you will not mind, because, as everybody knows, a woman is not as ambitious as a man, and besides you do not need the money so badly because your husband also earns. In addition, you do not *deserve* as much as a man because you will probably drop out of academic life after a few years. Women also have the annoying habit of going on maternity leave and falling sick more often than men while at the same time having the audacity to live longer. These facts clearly argue against equal opportunity.

If, on the other hand, you belong to a "minority group" —if you are a Jew, a Puerto Rican, an Afro-American, or a foreigner—you are at a distinct advantage, and you should make the most of it. Academics are well-known to be liberals and free of vulgar prejudices. (Antifeminism does not count, and if you accuse any colleague of it, he will retort that his most intimate friend is a woman.) Academics are so extraordinarily sensitive to any imputation of racism, anti-Semitism, xenophobia, or what have you, that a minority-group person can easily blackmail himself into a promotion. In fact, in most cases, he will not even need to do so, because his WASP colleagues will gladly apply a double standard without any prompting on his part. Everybody wants a black face on the staff, and there are not enough to go around. Jews are, of course, not in short supply in academia, so the advantage of being one is not as great as being an Afro-American, but on the other hand, anti-Semitism is so heinous a crime that a little discreet blackmail can go a long way. Such are the blessings of living in a racist society.

Foreigners are the darlings of academe. Every department wants to have a reputation for urbanity and cosmopolitanism. Exoticism is a prized commodity, at least at better schools. (Mediocre schools may still exhibit a kind of corn-belt or Bible-belt provincialism, but that, of course, is one of the reasons why they remain mediocre.) It is no accident that most foreign academics in America remain conspicuously, indeed sometimes belligerently, unassimilated. They are simply capitalizing on their exoticism. Until recently, this role was reserved to Europeans, who represented a cultural role model for the upwardly mobile academic snob. Now that the brain drain has extended to the "developing" countries, a variety of Indians, Pakistanis, Nigerians, and others have widened the range of not-so-local color represented on American campuses. Provided such persons have degrees from recognized institutions, they are in great demand, and if they happen to be dark-skinned, they have really got it made.

»» 6 ««

Teaching: What to do About It

Teaching is a necessary evil and an annoying distraction from more profitable ventures. One of the basic problems the successful academic must solve is how to escape the following vicious circle: The lowlier one's status, the heavier one's teaching load; and the more one teaches, the less likely one is to rise in status. The less prestigious a college is, the more staggering its teaching load, and the lower one's rank is in a given institution, the more "contact hours" one has compared to one's colleagues. Yet it is the young assistant professor who most badly needs the time to do research and to write, so as to escape his humble station. To begin one's career with a high teaching load is analogous to trying to swim across the English Channel with a lead belt. Students are like barnacles: they cling to one and retard one's progress.

In theory, research and teaching are the twin activities to which a scholar should devote his studious existence, and, in theory again, he is supposed to be equally rewarded for excellence in both. Of course, everybody knows that the rewards go to those who do research and publish, while devotion to teaching seldom brings more than the opportunity to do a lot of it for little money.

There are several reasons why teaching goes unrewarded. The first is that it has to do with mere students, and since students are little more than a pretext for having universities, any position that brings you in contact with hordes of youthful philistines is regarded as inconsequential. The second reason is that your colleagues find it difficult to assess your teaching, because in most cases they have never heard you in a classroom.

The third reason why teaching matters so little is that academics strenuously resist accepting the evaluations of those best placed to judge teaching, namely the students. Of late, students have begun to realize that they could potentially wield some control over their teachers by publishing more or less truculent course critiques. However, under the present system where professors can still dismiss course critiques as impertinent pranks, teachers remain largely immune from the adverse consequences of their incompetence or laziness, or both.

One of the great advantages of the teaching profession over the "free" professions is that the teacher's income and position are completely independent of what his clients think of him. While lawyers, dentists, and physicians in private practice have achieved some success in preventing their victims from gaining an accurate perception of their competence or otherwise, they are still, in last analysis, dependent on the layman's satisfaction with the services he receives. That satisfaction is frequently ill-founded, and indeed success is in no small measure the reward of quackery, but, in the end, most professionals depend on the willingness of their victims to let themselves be fleeced.

The teacher is luckily spared that indignity, except in the charmingly obsolete and nearly defunct practice of a few German universities where lecturers' fees vary with the size of the audiences. On the whole, academic income and other rewards vary inversely with the number of students. The more insufferably boring your courses, and the fewer your students, the more leisure you have to publish, and the better off you are. Small classes can perhaps wound the vanity of those few professors who think of themselves as great teachers, but never their pocketbooks. Besides, you can always claim that students avoid your courses not because your courses are dull, but because they are difficult.

There is a notable exception, however, to the irrelevance of teaching to a professor's career. One of the more useful myths of academia is that there tends to be an inverse relationship between good teaching and good research. It is true, of course, that very few professors excel in both, but it should be equally obvious that most professors are quite mediocre (and quite a few downright incompetent) in both activities.

Nevertheless, the presumption often remains that if a colleague is not capable of producing publishable research, he must therefore be an able and devoted teacher, and hence an asset to the university. The case of the experimental genius who is reduced to an incoherent mumbler in the classroom, or whose intellect so towers over that of his fellow mortals that he finds it impossible to bring himself down to earth, is an exceedingly rare specimen indeed. By and large, professors who do good research are also reasonably good in teaching and vice versa.

Why then the myth? Almost every department has a few distressing cases of weak or lazy colleagues whose incompetence at research and publication has been amply demonstrated, but who are nevertheless such nice chaps that one would like to see them promoted. Far and away the best method of doing so is to invoke their unproven, and, happily, unprovable, excellence in the classroom.

There are basically four types of teachers with four corresponding styles of classroom performance:

Type One: Those who love both teaching and students.
Type Two: Those who love teaching but hate students.
Type Three: Those who hate teaching but love students.
Type Four: Those who hate both teaching and students.

1) The first type is characteristic of the young assistant professor who has not yet had the time to become bored with his subject and disgusted about his students' anti-intellectualism. Happily, this set of attitudes seldom survives five years of abrasive contacts with students, but, while it lasts, it can do considerable damage to a young professor's career. Popularity-mongering is the lecturing style corresponding to that syndrome. With the neophyte's enthusiasm, many a young assistant professor polishes his lectures, practices them on his wife (or, more mercifully, in front of a mirror), and does his best to make them lively, dynamic, interesting, relevant to his students' life experiences, not too abstract and "academic," and interspersed with mildly salacious jokes. He regards students as idealistic, progressive, identity-searching youths who look to him as an elder brother leading them up the garden path of truth in a friendly, comradely fashion.

The dangers of this approach are obvious. To take one's

lecturing seriously can be so time-consuming as to leave no time for anything else. The conscientious young professor may in extreme cases devote to each lecture as much preparation time as his rivals do to a journal article, but with widely discrepant consequences. The neophyte's vanity may bask for a while in his facile classroom successes, but he is in fact walking headlong on the path to academic Alaska. The danger of devoted teaching is compounded by the fact that such lovers of students, in their eagerness to attract large audiences, are also lenient in their grades and accessible to their charges.

Their courses get known as "mickeys" (or whatever the current argot might be); their enrollments grow alarmingly; and their offices are assaulted by hordes of unscrupulous young barbarians seeking recognition, attention, solutions to their love affairs, or loans of money. The little time they can spare from lecture preparation is eaten up listening to students' problems. Three to five years later, the no-longer-so-young assistant professor is politely shown the door of his university with a suggestion that his teaching talents would receive greater recognition in a more modest institution that specializes in the lavish dispensation of personal attention to students. His long-haired coterie of progressive students may stage a little demonstration in his support in front of the dean's office and write a couple of letters to the student daily, but in the end he must pack his bags for some obscure and bucolic little college tucked away in the pinewoods of Maine, Pennsylvania, or Oregon, bemoaning the ingratitude of his colleagues and embittered about the unrewarding character of academic life.

The poignancy of his plight is that, at the very moment

he is beginning to hate teaching, he has irrevocably engaged himself on the road to academic mediocrity where research is well-nigh impossible and heavy teaching loads unavoidable. For the remaining twenty-five or thirty years of his career, he will belong to the unhappiest category of academics: the Type Four teacher who missed his chance at the big league because he once loved teaching.

2) The Type Two teacher, the person who enjoys teaching but dislikes students, represents one of the more successful adaptations to the academic environment. He is the person who, because of his verbal fluency, likes to hear himself talk, especially to large and attentive audiences. The teacher with a gift for rhetoric and a flair for histrionics will not only find teaching enjoyable but often will be quite effective in the classroom as well. His verbal facility will spare him the necessity of spending much time preparing his lectures. A few phrases hastily jotted down ten or fifteen minutes before the lecture will do the trick. Or he may even extemporize his way through. Thus his precious time, unlike that of his Type One colleague, is not diverted from the more profitable channels. With little effort, he passes for a good lecturer, superficial though his treatment often is.

However, to be completely successful, the Type Two teacher must devise techniques to repel the students who might find his classroom manners enticing. Condescension, irony, and superciliousness are very effective means of making students hate, or at least fear, you, and hence of freeing yourself of their importunities. The more you cut the student down to size, the less you will see of him.

The main drawback of the Type Two approach is that, in order to be carried off successfully, it requires considerable self-confidence and talent. Failing that, your more perceptive students will call your bluff, and the attempt may end in humiliation. The professor who lacks the necessary histrionic and rhetorical gifts will find the Type Four solution safer though devoid of brio. The successful Type Two lecturer is frequently a campus prima donna because his verbal fluency makes him also a prolific writer, a public speaker much in demand in other universities, a well-known polemicist, in short a shining star of academe. Seldom does he make profound contributions to knowledge, but if his counterfeiting of scholarly currency is glittering enough, very few people will ever know the difference, least of all the colleagues who will promote him.

3) Type Three makes a sad contrast with Type Two. Here are found those pathetic figures who would like to be popular with students but to whom teaching is a traumatic ordeal because they lack self-confidence, are paralyzed by stage fright, or suffer from some speech impediments. No matter how hard they try, their lectures are boring, incoherent, and confusing. They spend as much time as Type One in preparing their lectures, but they do not have the satisfaction of basking in student popularity. They are the dull, nice fellows who never dare ask for a salary raise, who get promoted very slowly, but who nevertheless serve the useful functions of reducing their colleagues' teaching load and setting off their brilliance by contrast.

The lecture style (if one may use this term) corresponding to this type is the shy, modest, unassuming delivery made in a barely audible monotone, full of hesitations, clumsy constructions, and dangling sentences. Equally painful to the speaker and to the audience, such courses are best scheduled at 8 A.M. when one still has a good excuse for persistent yawning. Type Three is a beginner's syndrome, and may with appropriate therapy blossom into Type Four.

4) Finally Type Four, while it lacks the brio of Type Two, avoids the fatal pitfalls of Type One and the indignities of Type Three. In short, the Type Four teacher represents the norm to which most academics should strive, and which in fact most attain within five years of getting their Ph.D.'s. It represents an unglamorous but basically sound adaptation to the demands of academic life.

The Type Four teacher regards teaching as an annoying distraction from research and writing, and students as an evil necessary to justify his job in the eyes of the laymen who directly or indirectly pay his salary. His major aim is to spend as few hours in the classroom as possible, and to discourage as many students as possible from taking his courses. He keeps his classes small by giving dull, abstract, pedantic lectures in a crisp, matter-of-fact tone, by behaving in an authoritarian manner, by discouraging questions and class discussions, and by being stingy with grades. To minimize waste of time in preparation of lectures, the same course is given year after year. The course may even be mimeographed and distributed, thereby making physical presence in the classroom a purely perfunctory ritual.

Refinements on this style include the cultivated ability to finish lectures at the precise moment when the bell rings, and the cracking of jokes at carefully prearranged places. The important thing is to leave the student no doubt that the lecture is a purely mechanical one that scarcely if at all involves the intellect of the professor. Ideally, the professor must behave as if he were a videotape recording of himself. This will make the transition to the close-circuit televersity of the future a smooth one, when professors and students will be spared the necessity of ever meeting face-to-face.

It should be clear from the above that avoidance of teaching beyond the unavoidable minimum is the prime condition of success in an academic career. There is however a quaint and vestigial exception to that rule. For historical reasons, the mainstream of academic life is supposed to involve *some* teaching. It follows that positions which do not normally entail teaching (e.g., administrative jobs, research institute posts, or positions in the foundations) generally have lower or at least more insecure status than straight academic jobs with their professorial titles. Nobody quite knows what it means to be a "research associate" or "senior research fellow" in an institute. It could mean anything from a first-year graduate student to a person with twenty years of post-doctoral experience. But to be an associate professor at such-and-such a university places you fairly precisely on a dual ladder of academic rank and of institutional prestige.

Since a professor has to do at least a token amount of teaching, it follows that many deans, directors of research institutes, foundation executives, and the like are eager to hold a regular professorship as well, and thus to do a token amount of teaching to "keep their hand at it" and convince their mainstream colleagues that they are still bona fide academics.

University professors are very adept at not letting the public know how little they teach. Most taxpayers still believe that the staff at the state university teach twenty to twenty-five hours a week, while, in fact, they teach about one fourth that amount. Fifteen-hour loads that were common some ten or twelve years ago have been gradually whittled down to twelve, then to nine. By now, the top schools regard six hours a week as a maximum, and their more senior staff get by with an average of three or four hours a week in the classroom. Anything over six hours indicates that you are a poor bargainer or that you belong to a second-rate institution, and anything over nine hours puts you in academic Alaska.

State legislatures can sometimes be embarrassingly inquisitive about teaching loads in public institutions. But as in other professions, teachers can easily pull the wool over laymen's eyes. The story goes of a professor testifying before a legislative committee. When asked by a state representative how many hours he taught, he replied in all honesty, "Eight." Whereupon, the legislator was visibly satisfied and commented, "At least you put in an honest day's work." The professor, of course, meant *per week.*

Many state universities still claim to have a twelve-hour load while in fact they get away with half. A variety of effective devices are used to maintain that fiction. One of the best is to assign to each professor a certain number of inactive graduate students who are supposedly taking "thesis guidance" or "reading courses," but who, like Gogol's serfs in *Dead Souls,* scarcely ever show up. Another device is to have graduate teaching assistants ghost teach for the most senior staff. For a mere pittance of some $3000 a year, hungry assistants on half-time will in fact teach as much as professors on full-time, and therefore nicely inflate on paper the latter's teaching load when departmental averages are computed. In the most favorable cases, teaching assistants, not being members of the regular staff, will appear on he debit side as students in teacher-student ratios, while heir teaching will be credited to members of the full-time taff. Any dean worth his salt should be able to think of at east six different ways of manipulating statistics to hide he facts from laymen.

The inverse relationship between quantity of teaching nd quality of school is not accidental. The two factors are ausally related. The best staff are attracted by the schools hat can offer the lowest teaching loads; a low teaching load neans an opportunity to do research and publish; and this n turn enhances the prestige of both the individual and the nstitution. Conversely, the poor chap who has to accept heavy load at a mediocre school will never produce much printed output, and both he and his institution can look orward to a shared future of obscurity and mediocrity.

Even within a given institution, an astute person can levise ways of reducing his load to something below the verage in his department. The following are just a few uggestions:

1) Try to get the highest level of courses you can, gradu- te seminars being the best possible. This has a dual advan- age. High-level courses have smaller enrollments because hey are more specialized, and they are easier to teach specially if they are in your speciality. A graduate seminar n your field requires little if any preparation at all. You just listribute a reading list, assign topics to your students, let hem do most of the talking, and confine your activities to wo or three wise remarks a week. Unfortunately, senior professors are well aware of the advantages of graduate eminars and tend to monopolize them, so this leaves little cope for the young assistant professor.

2) Volunteer to take charge of the large introductory

course. You will normally have little competition for the job, and your colleagues will take you for a fool, but do not let this bother you. First, you will be able to argue that the course is so large that by itself it constitutes a full load. Your colleagues will be so glad not to have to teach it, that they will readily concede the point, and your formal teaching will be limited to two or three hours a week, repeatable year after year. The number of students (which may run into the thousands) is actually quite irrelevant because you will be given a squad of teaching assistants to take charge of the sections and to mark the papers and examinations. In any case, you would give electronically marked multiple-choice exams.

There are two added advantages to controlling the introductory course. It makes you the biggest employer of graduate students in the department and hence gives you much power over them. And, should you decide to write a textbook, it gives you an assured market no matter how bad your book is.

3) Suggest that you share a course with a colleague, and argue that the course will be so much the better if students are exposed to two different but complementary points of view. This device automatically cuts lecturing in half for the course, and yet each of you gets credit for a full course.

4) Allow for a lot of discussion in class. This is fashionable and popular with students whom you give the illusion of freedom to express themselves. You have to be prepared to take a certain amount of criticism gracefully, but difficult or embarrassing questions can always be thrown back to the class. As most students prefer listening to their own drivel, there is no reason why you should not oblige for a

least half of the time. You will pass for a pioneer of progressive thinking, compete with the "free" universities off campus, and have to devote little time in preparing your lectures. Be careful, however, to avoid the pitfalls of political activism and student popularity. Both are very time-consuming and seldom profitable.

5) Give your teaching assistant a chance to deliver a few lectures. He is probably eagerly waiting for the opportunity, will feel flattered that you have asked him, and will spend so much time preparing his lectures that he is likely to do at least as good a job as you. Thus he gains experience, you gain leisure, and the undergraduates will probably enjoy seeing a new face.

6) Try to organize a symposium type of course to which you invite your colleagues to give one or two lectures each in their specialties. For each of them, it only means one or two extra hours of work, and that device spares you practically a whole course. Furthermore you will acquire the reputation of being an innovative teacher, and of being tolerant of a wide variety of points of view.

7) Get a joint appointment with two departments if you can, and play one against the other. The product of your two half-loads should be a one-fourth load.

8) Get research grants that will buy you time off from teaching and give you paid summer vacations in addition. All you have to do in return is research, which you can then use to get more grants to do yet more research and less teaching.

A judicious combination of the above methods can whittle down your teaching load to virtually nothing, and win you a reputation as a progressive and effective teacher to boot. This calls, of course, for a certain amount of finesse.

Affect an interest in teaching in early career stages. A blasé or cynical attitude toward teaching is one of the many privileges which come only with tenure. Affectation of sophistication by premature deprecation of teaching is dangerous for an assistant professor unless he is brilliant but here again the odds are unfavorable.

On the other hand, do not overdo your professions of interest in the students. Enthusiasm could be correctly interpreted as insincerity, or incorrectly attributed to hetero- or homosexual proclivities. Benevolent and condescending interest in students combined with decorous distance is perhaps the most appropriate stance for the assistant professor hoping for tenure. This stance also has the advantage of repelling students, and hence of leaving the young professor enough time to write.

Should you be afflicted with a genuine interest in students, remedial therapy should include frank discussions of your predicament with well-disposed colleagues. Should this fail, try at least to exploit students by making them collect data or even ghost-write articles.

We suggested earlier in this chapter that most professors regard teaching as a necessary evil. I have tried to show that, with a little initiative and imagination, teaching is no even as necessary as it might first seem. Attacked on the right by the spectre of videotapes and Skinner boxes, and on the left by free universities and student discussion groups, university teaching is becoming more and more vestigial anyway. Soon the dream of many professors, a university where students are nothing more than a decorative *tableau vivant* of fluttering miniskirts, may come into being. Conservative students will faithfully take in their daily dose of canned, televised lectures in the air-condi tioned comfort of their rooms; radical students will divide their time between hygienic picketing of administration buildings and soul-searching orgies of free discussions in smoke-filled cellars; and professors will publish even more than they do now, an all-important activity to which we must now turn our attention.

7

Publishing: How to Do It*

Publication of research, we are told, is the scholar's main contribution to science and society. With rare though notable exceptions, scholarly publication does not have any beneficial consequences for anybody except the author and his nuclear family, a handful of typographers and printers, and the shareholders of paper mills. These conditions explain both the low quality of the printed output, and the popularity of publication among authors, especially college professors. In fact, publishing has become a compulsion. The average academic author does not write because he has something to say, because he hopes to contribute to knowledge, or because he has fun doing it; rather, he writes and publishes in order to improve his *vita.* This document is frequently the only thing about him which his colleagues will ever read; it is the passport to academic success; and, beyond the routine acquisition of a Ph.D., published titles are the main ornament of a *vita.*

* This chapter was first published as an article in *Mawazo,* 2, 1969, and permission to reprint is gratefully acknowledged.

Scholarly publication is thus an extremely elaborate and patient exercise in *vita* construction.

The gamesmanship of publication involves a set of difficult dilemmas which lurk in the subconscious of many players, but are seldom explicitly stated. Let us turn to some of these problems:

1) *Quantity versus Quality*

For most people, of course, this problem never arises, because quality is beyond their reach. But insofar as a real dilemma exists, the optimum strategy of Scholarly Status Maximization (SSM) is clear. Rush into print, at least in the early stages of your professional career. For one thing, you have no reputation to lose. For another, most people who are instrumental in hiring or promoting you will never read anything you wrote besides your *vita.* Consequently, quality of publication is almost completely irrelevant to career chances.

There are three partial exceptions to this strategy, however:

a) A profession of concern for quality can be advanced as a rationalization for not publishing at all. This can be a very useful time-buying device for hard-pressed young assistant professors, because most academics still recognize the theoretical possibility that masterpieces occasionally take a few years to write. But the effectiveness of this device decreases drastically after three or four years, and at best it carries the assistant professor over the hump of his first contract renewal. Almost any department prefers you to publish trash rather than not publish at all. As a deterrent against publishing manuscripts which lay dormant in your filing cabinets, concern for quality is laudable in the abstract but foolish in practice, except in the two following special cases:

b) Publishing beyond a certain amount can be regarded as excessive. The best SSM strategy is to adjust for the average productivity of the department where the author hopes to stay. If his rate exceeds the departmental average by a substantial and painfully embarrassing margin, pressures against "rate-busting" are brought to bear against him. Arguments are then advanced that if you publish so much it cannot possibly be any good, and you may have to change jobs. The prudent untenured faculty member should thus endeavor to publish only slightly more than his competitors, or, should he be a rate-buster, he should conceal the fact and use his "excessive" publications only for purposes of negotiations with outside schools. This may require the production of a special toned-down *vita* for internal consumption.

c) The marginal utility of any given publication for SSM decreases as the size of your bibliography increases. E.g., while your first book, even if it does not sell, probably adds at least $50,000 to your life income, your fifth book will have only an imperceptible effect on your salary. It follows that once you have attained the status of full professor on the strength of a sizable bibliography, the marginal utility of further publications is minimal. In fact, if you attain national stature, it is probably best to stop publishing altogether, on the ground that your reputation can only decline by further exposure to intellectual scrutiny. Your own graduate students may lull you into a false sense of security by loudly proclaiming your infallibility, but younger colleagues at other universities can make a career out of attacking you, and by now you have become a tantalizing target. Further publication thus becomes dysfunctional to SSM.

There is also an intellectual reason for discontinuing publication by the time you are a full professor. By then, the chances are that your IQ has seriously deteriorated. This should not be a cause for undue alarm; with the proliferation of administrative jobs, you can still serve a useful and decorous function as chairman or dean.

2) *Prestigeful versus Obscure Outlets*

The neophyte would hardly consider this a dilemma. Does it not stand to reason that he should try to place his prose with the most prestigious journals or publishers? For the beginner, this strategy may commend itself. Your colleagues will rarely read your prose, but they will often weigh your bibliography in terms of the prestige of the journals where you publish.Beyond your first faltering steps as an assistant professor, however, the optimum strategy calls for publishing in obscure journals (POJ). At the risk of belaboring the obvious, the reasons for the POJ strategy are as follows:

a) Nowadays, anyone who can tell an IBM card from a Social Security card can practically be assured of getting articles published in "prestige" scholarly journals. This means that little prestige accrues from publishing as such. What counts is whether other people quote you. If you do publish in "prestige" journals, you are almost inevitably quoted, but this deflates the prestige value of the quotation. Although being quoted is more prestigious than merely publishing, reference to a well-known journal clearly confers less prestige to both the quoting and the quoted author than reference to a recondite source. After all, even college sophomores now read the leading journals, but only real scholars publish in and read the *Proceedings of the Jamaican Society for the Advancement of Science.* The more obscure the quotation, the more prestigious it is to quoter and quoted alike.

b) What happens, you may ask, if you do not get quoted? You still win. The odds are heavily in favor of somebody else writing the same article, or at least one on a closely related topic within five years. If he writes the same article and does not quote you, you write a rejoinder to the journal where he published his piece, and you kill two birds with one stone:

1) You expose him as a plagiarist and establish yourself as a superior scholar.
2) You add a title to your bibliography.

If the person who does not quote you merely writes in the same area but differs with you in his approach, you follow the same procedure and merely substitute for the charge of plagiarism one of poor scholarship or incompetence. This can also be quite devastating. Foreign language journals have an added advantage besides obscurity. If your colleagues ignore them, they are obviously ethnocentric philistines, and, though this label aptly describes many American scholars, the charge is still regarded as a serious one. Most of your colleagues have once passed their language exams and thus regard themselves as cosmopolites, while delighting in having somebody else exposed as an untutored boor.

In addition to SSM, POJ also has some monetary incentives. Obscure journals often still indulge in the charmingly obsolescent practices of sending their contributors an honorarium, free subscriptions, and free reprints.

3) *Articles versus Books*

The number of books published in a given field is inversely related to the intellectual sophistication achieved in that field. Very few books are written in physics, mathematics, or chemistry; a great many in political science, sociology, education, and home economics. This fact should not deter a scholar to write books if he belongs to a discipline in which many books are written. In fact, SSM dictates a prolific and verbose output if such is the characteristic of the field.

Especially useful in this connection is the inflation of an article into a book. Once upon a time, scholars condensed their 500-page dissertation into one or two ten-page articles, usually with little if any loss in content. Now, the successful academic in the verbose fields blows up a ten-page article into a 500-page book. However, this practice is not as bad as it sounds, because in many cases he will also publish under different titles half-a-dozen articles which repeat each other as well as the content of the book. One still needs to read only one article, or its abstract, if that much. Should the professor in a verbose field yet have to publish a book in order to get tenure, he always can (and usually does) resort to assembling the works of his colleagues into a book of readings. In doing so, he flatters the ego of the persons whose works he reprints, increases his reputation, and earns royalties. Books of readings always have an assured market: They are widely assigned in the classes taught by the authors whose works are republished. But, as we shall see presently, one should be wary of writing best-sellers.

The professor who belongs to a discipline where book writing is frowned upon, should, of course, refrain from doing so himself, or use a *nom de plume* to protect his scholarly identity, or wait until late in his career, if vanity impels him to sign his own name to his book. An aging mathematician or physicist who is no longer bright enough to contribute crisp little two-page gems to the professional journals may be excused for writing lengthy books on nuclear disarmament or high-school education. Physicists and mathematicians even derive a malicious pleasure in noting that colleagues in their dotage often write better books in fields outside their competence than expert social scientists, "educationists," or humanists do at their prime in their own specialties. Bertrand Russell once remarked that, as his intelligence gradually deteriorated, he successively turned from mathematics, to physics, to sociology, and finally to politics. Of course, it might be said in defense of statesmen that they are generally well past their prime when they achieve power. By the time they write their memoirs, they have typically attained the absolute nadir of human intellectual achievement.

4) *Commercial versus University Presses*

The obvious solution would be to favor commercial publishers on the grounds that they offer higher royalties and reach a wider market because they are actually interested in selling books, which university presses are not. But this is a very naïve view of publication gamesmanship. On at least ninety five per cent of all books published by professors, the author earns far more in increased salary than he ever will on royalties. A first book is worth at least $2,000 in annual salary increment until retirement age, while royalties seldom bring in more than $500 to $1,000 a year for two or three years. Thus, considerations of royalties and distribution are secondary. To maximize the sale of your book can even be dangerous. Indeed, there is an inverse correlation between how widely a book is read and how highly it is esteemed by your colleagues. Should your book be so unfortunate as to become a best-seller, your colleagues will debunk you as a journalist, an amateur, a dilettante, or—and this is a very damaging insult—a "popular" author. University presses will effectively protect you against this fate through a combination of prohibitive pricing, lack of advertisement, and absence of distribution.

If you cannot refrain from writing something which others might enjoy reading, use a pseudonym. It is the appropriateness of this strategy which lends any plausibility to theories that Francis Bacon would have used a pseudonym if indeed he ever penned such frivolous pieces of mass culture as *Macbeth*, *King Lear*, and *Hamlet.* Why indeed should he have wanted to compromise his solid reputation as the author of the *Novum Organum*, a work sublimely beyond the grasp of all but a few hundred of his contemporaries? By the same logic, the authorship of *Gone with the Wind* may be attributed to Einstein in the 24th century.

There is one exception to the taboo against writing best-sellers, namely textbooks. A successful textbook adds little to your scholarly status, and even less to the sum of human knowledge, but it can add a great deal to your income, and it seldom damages your reputation. To be sure, some haughty academics sneer at textbook writers, but such people can be dismissed as envious of the man who just financed a swimming pool, a third car, or a 30-foot yacht by writing *The Fundamentals of Home Cooking and Budgeting.* Textbooks escape the scholarly opprobrium of other best-sellers because they are in fact a very special kind of best-seller. Unlike all others, they are not bought by choice or for pleasure.

Textbooks are academically respectable because they are so tedious, and because the superficially incriminating sales figures in no way reflect the popularity of the book. The most successful textbooks are those written by teachers of large introductory courses at multiversities. With enrollments at your own school running into the thousands each year, and royalties averaging one dollar per copy, your book will do quite well even if no other professor adopts it. Textbook sales in the tens of thousands typically mean that twenty to fifty professors like the book, or that, in the absence of any good textbooks, they picked one at random. Surely, no sane person would misconstrue this as a measure of popularity. Confronted with a malevolent colleague who accuses you of being a popular writer, you will always be able to quote a review of your textbook which perceptively notes that your work is dull and pedantic.

5) *Concentration versus Dispersion*

The common-sensical thing, of course, would seem to be to spead one's publications in many different journals so as to reach a broader public. This might be termed the "hippopotamus technique" after the winning habit of these pachyderms to mark their territory when on land by quickly rotating their tails while defecating, and thereby spreading their telltale droppings. Early in one's career, this technique is not efficacious, due to the overabundance of scholarly hippopotamuses. Besides, publication dispersal may open one to charges of eclecticism, marginality to the discipline, and the like. By contrast, the "rhinoceros technique"—i.e., the rapid accumulation of a strategically located pile—is frequently more visible in early career stages. The hippopotamus technique, like POJ, is introduced later in one's professional existence.

6) *To Quote or Not to Quote*

Quotations and footnotes are generally regarded as *prima facie* evidence of scholarship. So there is no question that one should use footnotes.[1] An additional advantage of quotations and footnotes is that they are the least expensive way of flattering the ego of your colleagues, thereby, through the operation of reciprocal narcissism, greatly improving their evaluation of you. Through a process as yet imperfectly understood, references almost invariably come to the attention of the quoted author. (One plausible explanation is that many scholars spend much of their time

[1]. I take this opportunity to report that the editors of five scholarly journals rejected this chapter when I submitted it for publication as an article. Lack of space was the most commonly mentioned ground for rejection, with the implication that a serious journal should not waste its precious columns of fine print on frivolous pieces such as this one. Scholarly prose, obeying a Parkinsonian law, expands to fill the space provided by journals. I would also like to think that, according to a Greshamian law, bad prose drives out the good.

scanning journals and book indices for references to their works.)

The neophyte must, however, be warned of the danger inherent in referring to the works of others. You enhance their status and hence exacerbate competition. Therefore, excepting references to your own work, footnoting must be strictly limited to persons who are clearly your seniors or your juniors. The latter are, interestingly, the more efficacious source of quotations for three reasons:

a) Your juniors are likely to be unknown, and the footnote thus becomes positively loaded with obscurity value.

b) By quoting, say, from a doctoral dissertation written under your fatherly guidance, you establish your relative seniority.

c) Over-quotation of your own mentors is often regarded as an indication of lack of independence and unsatisfactory resolution of the academic Oedipus complex.

7) *Readability versus Jargon*

In theory, jargon is a useful, indeed an occasionally elegant, shorthand device for the precise expression of complex ideas. In practice, it is most frequently used as a mask for intellectual pedantry and poverty. This is the sense in which jargon is a precious adjunct to most scholarly careers. Three caveats must be introduced, however:

a) Sometimes even the most skillful use of jargon cannot protect vacuous statements from embarrassing exposure by ill-disposed colleagues. In such cases, a more readable statement might, to be sure, have aroused their scorn but not their sarcasm.

b) Excessive use of freshly coined jargon is sometimes interpreted as a mark of the neophyte's youthful enthusiasm for the cult language. This, of course, shows lack of maturity. The more mature scholar only uses well-established, seasoned jargon, which frequently is not quite jargon any more.

c) If you do have something original and important to say, and if you are still capable of saying it in readable form after undergoing graduate training, your writing is bound to attract attention through its novelty. The difficulty, of course, is that you are a poor judge of whether you have anything important to say—in fact, the odds are against you. A skillful use of seasoned jargon is the most prudent course.

8) *To Plagiarize or Not to Plagiarize*

The printed output of academics falls in four broad and overlapping categories:

a) Tediously footnoted rehash of the works of others. This probably accounts for 60 percent of the output. Such books and articles comprise a category which is accepted as both legitimate and competent, but it has the drawback of being excruciatingly boring.

b) Unwitting restatement of other works. This type of writing accounts perhaps for another 30 per cent. It is regarded as poor scholarship if detected.

c) Outright plagiarism. This accounts perhaps for some 9 per cent of the printed output. Plagiarism was once completely accepted. Bach, for example, shamelessly pirated Vivaldi, but then he was under tremendous publication pressure, having to produce something like a concert a week. Besides, he had many sons to feed, and it was some years before they started helping him out. Today plagiarism is frowned upon, but undetected plagiarism can be quite useful to the less imaginative professor who wishes to establish a claim to creativity.

d) Original ideas. These take at best 1 per cent of the printed space, and may be disregarded here as an insignificant residual category to be mentioned only for the sake of completeness.

Actually, the practice of plagiarism is not as risky as many beginning students may think. The dangers of plagiarism are inversely proportional to two factors: the academic seniority of the plagiarist, and the obscurity of the plagiarized source.

The second point is obvious. Only very stupid people plagiarize from well-known sources. Such people are likely to be eliminated from academia when they receive an F in their Freshman English Composition class. Quoting from *extremely* well known sources, however, is not considered plagiarism. One may lift passages from the Koran, the Bible, or the Declaration of Independence with impunity. If you are accused of anything it will not be of plagiarism, but rather of uttering clichés. Student papers, skilfully used, are the safest source of plagiarism, but, alas, they are seldom worth the trouble.

The dangers of plagiarism are also inverse to the academic seniority of the plagiarist. This is of little comfort to the beginning student who runs the highest risks when he stands to benefit most from the practice. To plagiarize with impunity is one more perogative of rank in the age-graded groves of academe. For the older professor in the throes of senile psychosis, plagiarism from the doctoral dissertations of his students can literally be a godsend. But even younger professors can safely plagiarize from their brighter graduate students. Should the student be foolhardy enough to confront his professor with the evidence, the charge is almost sure to boomerang. It will be assumed by all professors that the student got the idea from the professor in the first place. To facilitate plagiarism by professors, students are urged to make blanket intellectual acknowledgements to their teachers in the preface of their theses.

9) *Book Reviews*

This last important topic falls, strictly speaking, outside the scope of this chapter. Given the universal academic prejudice against authors writing critiques of their own books, those reviews about which one cares most fall largely outside one's direct control. This is unfortunate and could be remedied by initiating, for example, a system of self-criticism along Communist lines. Within thirty days of publication, say, each author would have to submit to the official organ of his discipline a critique of his book, which would be turned down by the editor until it reached an appropriate level of self-flagellation.

Under the present system, the control exercised by authors over reviews of their books is at best indirect. The safest strategy calls, of course, for the generous dispensation of undeserved praise in your reviews of colleagues' books. Generally, your colleagues will reciprocate. It is difficult not to think highly of somebody who thinks highly of you. At the very least, his judgment must be sound. Thus the foundations are laid for what historians of science call "schools of thought." Most fields of specialization are small enough for cozy little incestuous relationships to develop, wherein A reviews B's book and vice versa within the same issue of the same journal.

Nasty reviews are, of course, much more amusing to write and to read than complimentary ones, and they have the added merit of greater validity. However, the fear of retaliation restrains all but the most brilliant and senior academics. Most professors restrict their attacks against colleagues to the safety of their classrooms. All too seldom, a homeric battle of titans cutting each other to shreds with their devastating wit enlivens the pages of journals to the delight of graduate students who find in it invaluable material for their comprehensive examinations. But generally, alas, book reviews are nearly as dull as other genres of academic writing.

The victim of unfair reviews (and most truly witty reviews are unfair) should find solace in the fact that book sales seem unaffected by the quality of reviews. Bad reviews are better than no reviews at all. In the words of Chairman Mao, "the absence of attacks from the enemy is a bad thing." In the long run, everybody wins except the impecunious student who has to buy the blasted books.

Let us summarize the main rules of the publishing game. Like chess, the game can be broken into the opening, middle, and end phases:

a) Assistant professors should publish, preferably in prestige journals.

b) Associate professors should continue to publish, but preferably in obscure journals.

c) Full professors would often do well to become deans and stop publishing altogether.

A word of warning must be said, however, concerning "premature" publication by graduate students. This is a very touchy subject. Many professors regard premature publication by their students as an impertinence, unless the manuscript has received their *imprimatur*, and in most cases the addition of the professor's name as senior author. This practice is so common that, in coauthored papers where the order of the names is not alphabetical, the general presumption is that the "junior" author is in fact the sole one. The practice thus becomes self-defeating. Perhaps the day will soon come when professors will insist, for their self-protection, on their names appearing in alphabetical order.

The pressure on professors to publish is often said to create anxiety, to stifle creativity, and to encourage the production of a vast amount of trivia or worse. Journals are like proliferating repositories of academic night soil, which, far from fertilizing the ivory tower, slowly drown it in a steadily rising tide. It looks as if the hippopotamuses and rhinoceroses are slowly suffocating in their own waste. Stifling conditions, however, are not so much created by the quantity and quality of the output as by the deadly seriousness with which most professors take their publishing. Viewed as a game, publication is at least as entertaining as chess and no more unproductive. The present chapter, written at considerable risk to the author's reputation as a serious scholar, is a modest contribution in that direction.

»» 8 ««

Grants, Research, and Foundations

Scholarly works frequently are, or at least ought to be, the end product of research. Not that lack of research activity stops many academics from publishing all the same; but nearly all types of writing produced by academics, with the exception perhaps of "creative" writing, presuppose some kind of research in the field, the library, or the laboratory. Until the late 19th century, research was done on a very limited budget. Only a handful of people in the "hard" sciences could raise money from their governments or private benefactors, and even then only insofar as there existed a reasonable prospect of their coming up with a useful invention like a vaccine, a better cotton gin, or a more lethal artillery shell.

Happily, the situation has greatly improved, especially in the last thirty years. Public and private milch cows vie with each other to keep their coteries of academic retainers and to lubricate the scholarly printing plants. A huge research establishment has sprung up side by side with the universities and created an extraordinarily complex network of ties with them. Private foundations have proliferated thanks to a tax structure that makes philanthropy painless if not positively rewarding. The government got into the act through the National Science Foundation, through the research branches of its military machine, and through lavish contracts with private research corporations and universities.

Tens of thousands of scholars shuttle back and forth on leave of absence between government agencies, foundations, and universities; tens of thousands more work in independent or corporate research organizations; and many more yet do contract research at universities under government or foundation grants. It is this last category that shall concern us most here.

Not all disciplines are in an equally good position to milk the government and foundations. By and large, the "harder" the discipline is (i.e., the greater its demonstrated ability to deliver goods that are of interest to nonacademics), the better established its claim to spend vast chunks of the common weal. Physicists, especially since their resounding success in atomic pyrotechnics, have done best, followed by chemists, engineers, physicians, biologists, economists, psychologists, sociologists, and "educationists." The humanities have trailed far behind, but even they are now learning to dip their fingers into the pie.

There are a few odd cases that do not fit neatly into this continuum of grantability. For example, archeology, one of the softest and most gratuitous of sciences, has managed to develop around itself such a romantic aura as to attract substantial subsidies to unearth tons of pottery shards. The poorer a country is in terms of its present social conditions, the more eager it is to pay archeologists to dig up the glories of its past. Perhaps archeologists also know how to exploit statesmen's desire for immortality.

Conversely, mathematicians, although very hard, have a difficult time in convincing foundations that they need a lot of money since their end product is purely a figment of their imaginations. Now, fortunately, they are able to link their cogitations with expensive computer programs. And astronomy, one of the most exact of sciences, does not approach the ability of physicists to deliver the goods, and hence got a relatively modest share of research funds until the space program started boosting them in orbit. On the whole, however, natural scientists do best; social scientists are poor seconds; and humanists lag behind all others.

How has this academic raid on the public and corporate purse been organized? Basically, by creating the concept of "big research" as the necessary adjunct to "big government" and "big business." The old concept of the lone (and often self-taught) scientist making great discoveries in his cellar with twenty dollars' worth of products from the corner pharmacy, or a litter of mice from the pet shop, is hopelessly ridiculed as outdated. Today, Pasteur and Edison would be pitiable amateurs worthy at best of the Science Club at some provincial high school, and Marie Curie might perhaps just make it on the teaching staff, with a postgraduate refresher course at the State University.

Any worthwhile research, it is argued, must be a collaborative venture conducted by properly accredited scientists having access to the latest equipment. Specialization is so advanced that no man can have an adequate overview of a broad field, hence the need for team work and interdisciplinary research. Imagination counts for little, and method for much. Flashes of insight are to be mistrusted, and computers relied upon to hit on at least some pay dirt, if only because of their ability to dig up such vast quantities of rubbish. In fact, by chance alone, some five per cent of your tests will be statistically "significant" at the .05 level.

In the bad old days, when calculations had to be done with simple little desk machines or slide rules, when graduate assistants were scarce and resources limited, it paid to do some hard thinking, to develop sensible hypotheses, and to design well-controlled experiments. Today, when computers can intercorrelate hundreds of variables in seconds, hard thinking becomes redundant, indeed a hindrance to scientific progress. All you have to do is throw into the salad bowl anything that could conceivably be relevant to your vaguely formulated problem, dump this intellectual potpourri in the lap of a resentful computer programmer, browbeat him into doing what little thinking he can do for you, and wait for the "printout" to zigzag its way out of the gargantuan machine. The computer is a substitute for rigor and parsimony.

Research grants serve many useful and lucrative functions. They allow you to buy off half or more of your time from teaching, getting the latter down to two or three hours a week. They make it possible to attract and hire some of the best graduate students whose brains you can pick, with or without acknowledgement, in your research. Research grants can buy you secretarial assistance; in fact, short of being department chairman, grants are the only way to get a secretary all to yourself. Through research grants (which include 15 or more per cent overhead expenses given to the host university), you can commandeer a disproportionate amount of office and laboratory space.

In addition to paying part of your basic salary, grants will typically also give you an extra two months of summer salary. You can finance numerous jaunts to domestic and international conferences out of your research money without having to beg your university for it or having to justify your trip by reading a paper. And, if your research calls for going overseas, you can lead the life of an oriental potentate with an American income in a low-cost-of-living country. Should you remain an expatriate for eighteen months or more, you even get a $20,000-a-year income tax exemption for waiving the star-spangled banner from the halls of Montezuma to the shores of Tripoli.

The disadvantage of getting a research position in somebody else's institute has already been mentioned. The most advantageous course of action is to apply for a research grant of which you become the principal investigator while at the same time retaining your regular teaching, or rather, by now, your nearly nonteaching, post. Of course, research grants are not gotten for the asking. The successful applicant must show a number of qualities of which the principal one is probably intellectual dishonesty. This is especially true in the social sciences. This requisite dishonesty finds its purest expression in the formulation of the research proposal. To be successful, applications must not only follow certain routine procedures, meet deadlines, and be neatly filled out with the appropriate headings; they must also conform to certain fads, "standards," and prejudices which exist in the minds of the referees who evaluate the proposal and the committee that awards the grants.

Almost invariably, the scholars responsible for allocating

research funds on behalf of government and foundations belong to the establishment of their profession and tend to have the qualities of organization men. They are frequently the more cautious and conservative of the well-established political cosmopolites—not the creative scholars who earn their reputation through the quality of their work, but the persistent schemers who push themselves into positions of influence in their professional associations. Such people then nominate each other and their likes, and constitute within each discipline a loose interlocking directorate of big wheels belonging to the committees that count.

In drafting a research proposal, the primary concern should be to write it in such a way as to appear worthwhile to the evaluators rather than to give a candid description of what you intend or hope to accomplish; hence the need for dishonesty. Since intellectual dishonesty does not come easily to all academics, there is need for a few pointers:

1) Never give the impression that you do not know precisely what you want to do and how you are going to do it. This often involves dishonesty, because in the majority of cases you start a research project with only a general idea of what area you want to investigate and what methodology you want to use, and you have only a few hunches as to why you want to do it. Once you lay your hands on the money, you have a very wide degree of discretion how you actually spend it, but you will seldom if ever get money unless your proposal radiates serene self-confidence about what you propose to do.

2) Spell out in great detail your methodology and make it as quantitative and precise-looking as possible, even if

you know (as you should if you have any experience in research) that unforeseeable contingencies will almost certainly force you to modify your plans. You may also know that the rigor and precision which your design exudes are quite specious, because your proposal does not take field conditions into account; but these qualms should never deter you from giving the impression of great accuracy.

3) Use the proper style—i.e., avoid the first person singular, and if you must refer to yourself, use the third person and speak of yourself as "the principal investigator." Better yet, use the passive voice profusely—e.g., employ such phrases as "it is proposed to," "it will be seen whether." In short, the style should combine the qualities of the bureaucratic and the scholarly jargon to which your judges are accustomed: it should be impersonal, ponderous, pedantic, inelegant (a split infinitive here and there will do wonders), and, most of all, incomprehensible to laymen. Sometimes the application form will request you to state briefly your problem in nontechnical terms, but this is a crude booby trap. If you comply and write in lucid prose, what you want to do will often appear so simple as not to be worthy of support.

4) Survey the literature and try to anticipate who might review your proposal; then do not fail to quote their works. Failing that, try to suggest who your referee should be by profusely quoting the works of those whom you would like to read your application. The latter approach can, of course, boomerang if your proposal is sent to the wrong person.

5) Follow the fads of the day in your discipline. This will give the impression that you are up-to-date and adventuresome. Follow the fashion in jargon, theoretical ap-

proach, and methodology. Avoid true imaginativeness because the old whigs might define you as a crackpot, but through the clever verbal juggling of the "in" terms, create the illusion that creativity oozes out of every pore of your scalp.

6) Consult with foundation staff before filling out your application. Very often, they will give you the benefit of their experience and tell you what to say and how to say it in order to get your proposal through the various granting committees.

7) If the foundation you are applying to wants to believe that the research they are sponsoring is of some use to mankind, devote a couple of paragraphs to the practical or policy implications of your proposed research, even though you could not care less. At the same time, do not cast your project in too pedestrian terms, because many foundations want to support high-prestige, "pure" research, and not mere applied research. The precise formula to use should become apparent from foundation pamphlets, which, incidentally, are to be taken seriously, despite appearances to the contrary. Foundation executives are often the kind of persons who take an earnest view of themselves and their benefactors, and they are often authors of pamphlets explaining the aims of the foundation.

8) Pay careful attention to the budget part of the proposal, for it is an important one. A good budget must show two qualities: it must be both detailed and extravagant. A detailed budget shows that you have devoted some time to it. In this connection, avoid round figures which seem to be imprecise guesses. For example, do not state $1,000 for stationery and office supplies; instead say $975 or $1,025,

even though those figures are totally arbitrary. As to the second condition, it might seem to the beginner in the art of scholarly mendicity that the more modest one's demands are, the more likely they are to be satisfied. This is a grave fallacy; the very opposite is true.

In America, where what Thorstein Veblen called the pecuniary standards of excellence loom so large, no scientist is held to be worth much if he does not spend vast sums on his research, or at least if he does not have the audacity to make preposterous demands. Cheap research is held almost by definition to be inferior research, and the scientific disciplines themselves are ordered on a prestige scale that correlates very closely with how expensive they are. A nuclear physicist on a cyclotron is worth many Byzantine historians whose only research tools are books, and whose main research expense is a round-trip tourist fare to Istanbul.

A second reason why the probability of getting a grant is directly related to the amount asked for is that foundations and government agencies have large sums to give out, and that the smaller the number of grants is, the less work. Why burden yourself with giving 200 grants of $10,000 when you can painlessly dispend 20 grants of $100,000? The essential thing is that you demonstrate your ability to spend $2 million in a given period of time.

Nor are foundations deterred from giving large grants by the fact that, in many cases, the scientific returns are inversely related to funds expended. This is particularly true in the social sciences where the search for ways to inflate budgets has led scholars to complicated equipment of doubtful value, and to the massive use of computers, the sophistication of which has far outstripped the ability of social scientists to feed them with meaningful data.

There are numerous ways of inflating a research budget to get it more easily accepted. One can extend the time period, but most large grants are given for periods of three to five years, and this does not give one much flexibility. One can request a large staff of secretaries and assistants, but people have the serious disadvantage of requiring attention and supervision. One may run into the danger of becoming a mere administrator of a research organization, and of having no chance to do actual research and to publish. And publications, however trivial, are a precondition to getting further grants. Besides, salaries of ancillary personnel are fairly inelastic and do not allow for much padding.

Happily, there remain two items where the possibilities are virtually unlimited, namely equipment and computers. Even social scientists have become adept at making exorbitant demands for "small group laboratories," photographic and cinematographic equipment, tape recorders, and the like. Whole industries have developed to satisfy the extravagance of academic researchers.

In summary, the basic rules of successful grantsmanship are simple and quite like other types of merchandizing: Package your proposal in a way that will be attractive to the prospective donor, and put a high price tag on it so as to convince him that he is supporting excellence. A salable proposal should take approximately as much time to write as a journal article. It is also the most meretricious exercise in academia.

Do not be distressed, however, if your honesty and the quality of your work prevent you from getting research grants. Use your brain instead, and you will be surprised how good the results can be. Creativity, like love, cannot be purchased, and, like faith, it can still move mountains. You can do excellent research in many fields with little money. You can pretend to do research on no money at all. And remember that, in last analysis, your academic success depends not on whether you do research, but on whether you publish.

9

Conclusion

This book addressed itself to three "target audiences" (insofar as audiences can be bombarded as this military phraseology implies). Undergraduates about to take the fateful step of entering graduate school and thereby making at least a tentative commitment to academia will have to decide whether the academic game is worth playing. Before they conclude that it is not, however, I should like to suggest to them that the alternatives are scarcely any more appealing. Although political events of the last couple of years might seem to cast doubt on this statement, I still believe that the campus, threatened as it is, remains an island of comparative sanity and freedom in a generally repelling society. Graduate students who have already taken the crucial first step on the road to academia will have to decide whether to play the game or invest effort and creativity into changing the rules in greater conformity with their values. As to my professorial colleagues, the vast majority of them are too set in their ways, and their interests are too linked with the *status quo* to contemplate with equanimity any fundamental change. Buffeted on the left by the inchoate anger and romantic indignation of student "radicalism," and on the right by the bovine, satiated conservatism of the "silent majority" and the organized interests of the business, military and political "establishments," the vast majority of professors can be expected to react as a craft guild protecting their privileges. Their reaction to this book might range from annoyance to amusement, but before they put it down (and hopefully recommend it to their friends), they should at least ask themselves whether the system they created is still viable. Can a university which exists primarily for the benefit of its mandarins survive in a society that indulges in at least the rhetorical pretense of democracy?